CoursePrep
ExamGuide/StudyGuide
MCSE Exam #70-219

Designing a Microsoft Windows 2000
Directory Services Infrastructure

**COURSE
TECHNOLOGY**
™

THOMSON LEARNING

Australia • Canada • Mexico • Singapore • Spain • United Kingdom • United States

**COURSE
TECHNOLOGY**
™
THOMSON LEARNING

MCSE CoursePrep ExamGuide and *MCSE CoursePrep StudyGuide*
are published by Course Technology

Managing Editor
Stephen Solomon

**Senior Vice President,
Publisher**
Kristen Duerr

Production Editor
Brooke Albright/Trillium
Project Management

**Developmental
Editor/Product Manager**
Dave George

**Associate Product
Manager**
Tim Gleeson

Editorial Assistant
Nick Lombardi

Marketing Manager
Toby Shelton

Text Designer
GEX Publishing Services

Cover Designer
Elizabeth Young

TABLE OF CONTENTS

SECTION 3 DESIGNING A DIRECTORY SERVICE ARCHITECTURE ... 51

PREFACE

The *MCSE CoursePrep ExamGuide* and *MCSE CoursePrep StudyGuide* are the very best tools to use to prepare for exam day. These products are intended to be utilized with the core "Guide to" book, *MCSE Guide to Designing Microsoft Windows 2000 Directory Services* (ISBN 0-619-01689-2), written by Michael Palmer and published by Course Technology. *CoursePrep ExamGuide* and *CoursePrep StudyGuide* provide you ample opportunity to practice, drill, and rehearse for the exam!

COURSEPREP EXAMGUIDE

The *MCSE CoursePrep ExamGuide for Exam #70-219*, ISBN 0-619-03507-2, provides the essential information you need to master each exam objective. The *ExamGuide* devotes an entire two-page spread to each certification objective for the exam, helping you understand the objective and giving you the bottom-line information—what you really need to know. Memorize these facts and bulleted points before heading into the exam. In addition, there are several practice test questions for each objective on the right-hand page. That is hundreds of questions to help you practice for the exam! *CoursePrep ExamGuide* provides the exam fundamentals and gets you up to speed quickly. If you are seeking even more of an opportunity to practice and prepare, we recommend that you consider our total solution, *CoursePrep StudyGuide*, which is described below.

COURSEPREP STUDYGUIDE

For those really serious about certification, we offer an even more robust solution—the *MCSE CoursePrep StudyGuide for Exam #70-219*, ISBN 0-619-03473-4. This offering includes all of the same quality material you get with the *CoursePrep ExamGuide*, including the unique two-page spread, the bulleted memorization points, and the practice questions. In addition, you receive a password valid for six months of practice on CoursePrep, a dynamic test preparation tool. The password is found in an envelope in the back cover of the *CoursePrep StudyGuide*. CoursePrep is a Web-based pool of hundreds of sample test questions. CoursePrep exam simulation software mimics the exact exam environment. The CoursePrep software is flexible and allows you to practice in several ways as you master the material. Choose from Certification Mode to experience actual exam day conditions or Study Mode to request answers and explanations to practice questions. Custom Mode lets you set the options for the practice test, including number of questions, content coverage, and ability to request answers and explanations. Follow the instructions on the inside back cover to access the exam simulation software. To see a demo of this dynamic test preparation tool, go to *www.courseprep.com*.

FEATURES

The *MCSE CoursePrep ExamGuide* and *MCSE CoursePrep StudyGuide* include the following features:

Detailed coverage of the certification objectives in a unique two-page spread. Study strategically by really focusing in on the MCSE certification objectives. To enable you to do this, a two-page spread is devoted to each certification objective. The left-hand page provides the critical facts you need, while the right-hand page features practice questions relating to that objective. You'll find the certification objective(s) and sub-objectives(s) clearly listed in the upper left-hand corner of each spread.

An overview of the objective is provided in the ***Understanding the Objective*** section. Next, ***What You Really Need to Know*** lists bulleted, succinct core facts, skills, and concepts about the objective. Memorizing these facts will be important for your success when taking the exam. ***Objectives on the Job*** places the objective in an industry perspective and tells you how you can expect to incorporate the objective on the job. This section also provides troubleshooting information.

Practice Test Questions on each right-hand page help you prepare for the exam by testing your skills, identifying your strengths and weaknesses, and demonstrating the subject matter you will face on the exams and how it will be tested. These questions are written in a similar fashion to the real MCSE exam questions. The questions test your knowledge of the objectives described on the left-hand page and also the information in the *MCSE Guide to Designing Microsoft Windows 2000 Directory Services*. Answers to the practice test questions are found at the back of this Guide.

Case Studies: Certification objectives in this Guide are organized by topic area into different sections, as determined by Microsoft. Each section is prefaced by a case that presents a real-world security situation in a fictional company. Review questions in each situation will relate to this scenario.

Acronym Glossary: The world of networking, perhaps more than any other computer-related discipline, uses a language all its own, which is comprised largely of acronyms. You will find a complete list of all acronyms used in this Guide, along with their meanings, at the back of the book.

For more information: If you require more information about networking concepts in general, or MCSE exam objectives in particular, please see *MCSE Guide to Designing Microsoft Windows 2000 Directory Services*, by Michael Palmer (Course Technology, 2002).

Section 1

Analyzing Business Requirements

Coast Mortgage, Inc.

Coast Mortgage, Inc. is a large, regional mortgage lender specializing in the origination, approval, placement, and servicing of residential loans. They service their own loans as well as accept the servicing of loans closed by other lenders. They are active in the secondary mortgage market, buying and selling blocks of mortgages on a regular basis.

The company has two main divisions: loan servicing and sales. The loan servicing division handles all payment transactions for the loans it services. This includes processing the principal and interest payments and paying the taxes and insurance from escrow reserve accounts to the proper taxing authorities and insurance companies. The total number of loans serviced at any given time ranges from 65,000 to 75,000 with an average loan amount of $237,349. The types of loans being serviced run the gamut of conventional, FHA, VA, and those financed by state bond programs.

Coast has one headquarters office, two regional offices, and 35 branch offices, all located within the same state. The main server for the company is at corporate headquarters. A fractional T1 connects each regional office to headquarters, and a third fractional T1 provides Internet access for the regional offices and headquarters, as well as incoming VPN tunnels. Each regional office also has a server. Branch offices are connected to both regional offices and headquarters with a VPN tunnel over a 1 Mbps DSL link.

Each loan originator has a laptop computer on which they record all the pertinent loan information for each customer using industry standard, loan-generation software. From this loan application, the requisite Truth-in-Lending disclosures and other state and federal regulatory information are prepared. Each loan officer is responsible for getting the requisite signatures for proper processing of the loan at the time of the initial application. There are a very large number of federal and state rules and regulations that Coast Mortgage, Inc. is required to follow, as well as disclosures to prepare and distribute. All of this is managed at corporate headquarters by a custom program and takes into consideration not only new loans in process, but also the existing loan servicing portfolio. For each new loan they buy or sell, they are required to notify the mortgagee and provide contact information. The Sales Division handles this loan processing, which is done online beginning with the initial application. All reports and related items are ordered automatically, once the process is underway.

Each branch office is responsible for sending out the initial Truth-in-Lending disclosure within the requisite three-day window, although the regional office and corporate headquarters maintain oversight. The branch office is also responsible for generating all the materials for each loan, such as a credit report, appraisal request, home inspections as necessary, flood hazard determination, employment and deposit verifications, and other items, as the need arises. Home loans are a somewhat fluid and changeable commodity, although a certain formula exists. The monies collected as a deposit for the credit report and appraisal fees are deposited into a trust account managed by each branch office.

Once the loan is approved and any underwriting requirements are met, the loan is ready to close. Coast Mortgage has an escrow subsidiary that it frequently uses to close the transaction. Escrow companies have an entirely different set of laws, rules, and regulations with which they must comply. They receive the monies from the borrower, which they transmit to the closing financial institution, as well as the monies to pay the current lien holder, so that a new lien is created reflecting the purchase or refinance of the home. Reporting requirements are stringent. Settlement statements are prepared using standard, off-the-shelf software that contains the ability to collect and collate data for later reporting to the appropriate state and federal agencies. This is done monthly, quarterly, and annually.

Each company (mortgage and escrow) has a host of regulatory, reporting, and fiduciary responsibilities that are crucial to the continued success of the respective business. The ultimate responsibility for these operations is at corporate headquarters. They poll the servers at the regional office continually to collect data so that they know what is happening at any given moment. In addition, the servicing of the current loan portfolio is at corporate headquarters. This involves receiving and processing the payments for all the loans and properly accounting for the principal and interest payments as well and the tax and insurance information. At appropriate intervals, the tax and insurance payments are sent to the respective taxing authorities and insurance companies. In addition, periodic reports are prepared that show the performance of the portfolio for the companies, investors, and government regulators. Customer service is an entity unto itself, with a unique set of reporting requirements and duties. They must respond to a constant stream of customer requests and be ready to provide information to management, investors, the SEC, and a horde of other government entities, federal, state, and local.

The IT infrastructure quickly responds to all needs for information and equipment. The applications that each group uses are unique and are not compatible. The customer service software is proprietary. It is possible to export the information it generates to database application programs, but it does not directly communicate with the loan servicing software and investor reporting software. Investor and SEC reporting requirements demand a different format entirely.

The market is booming. Currently, the company serves a large metropolitan area, but right across the state line is a market with an even larger potential market base. The plan is to expand into this area with another regional office and two additional branch offices. As business increases, additional branch offices will open. Projections call for 10 additional branch offices in the next six months, if current trends continue. Before this expansion can happen, the network infrastructure must be upgraded.

Currently, the network is primarily running Windows NT throughout the company, but there are still a few loan officers that use Windows 98 on their laptops. Either they are too busy to upgrade, or they just have not gotten around to it. The plan is to upgrade everything to Windows 2000, with the corporate headquarters' servers using the Advanced Server version, regional offices using the Windows 2000 Server version, and the branch offices (loan officers included) using the Windows 2000 Professional version. Consideration is also being given to upgrading all fractional T1 lines to a full T1. Branches would continue using VPN tunnels, although L2TP and IPSec is being considered instead of the current PPTP.

Security has not been a problem, but concern is growing that more needs to be done. The firewall is software only at this point, but the CTO has been looking into a possible hardware and software combination that promises a more secure solution.

OBJECTIVES

1.1 Analyze the company model and geographical scope: regional, national, international, subsidiary, and branch office

REGIONAL • NATIONAL • INTERNATIONAL • SUBSIDIARY • BRANCH OFFICE

UNDERSTANDING THE OBJECTIVE

The company's organizational structure helps determine the AD design. If users are separated from the resources needed to perform their jobs, AD can make those resources appear local to the user.

WHAT YOU REALLY NEED TO KNOW

◆ The company's organizational chart helps explain the roles of the branches, regional offices, and headquarters. Network administration is of particular interest to help you understand the size, scope, and location(s) of the IT staff. If there is a large IT group in the company, it is most likely managed centrally. Do not forget about the IT needs of the regional offices and branches. This information plays a large role in both the logical and physical design of AD.

◆ Any situation representing a single point of failure may point to problems that can be resolved in the new AD environment.

◆ Consider the answers to the following questions to provide the basis for the AD design:
- Is there a corporate headquarters?
- Are there one or more centralized points of control (for example, regional offices)?
- Are the locations peers, superior/subordinates, partners, or competitors?
- Is the company a subsidiary or a holding company? What are the relationships to the other related companies? Will they all be migrating to AD?
- What group(s) manage access to the network and its resources (logically and physically)?
- What group(s) are responsible for desktop and server support and management?
- What level(s) of data security is/are required on the public and private networks?
- What are the primary resources on the network, and where are they located?
- Are links to other companies, contractors, and so on needed? If so, how will they be implemented (VPN vs. dial-up)?

OBJECTIVES ON THE JOB

Think about the interaction of the branches with the regional offices and headquarters in your organization. What is their interrelationship, and how do they work together? What are the IT needs of each department? Use this information to design your OU structure, tree, and forest design.

PRACTICE TEST QUESTIONS

Coast Mortgage wants to expand its operations across the state line. There are 35 branch offices at the moment, with an average of four sales staff, four assistants, a receptionist, and a manager in each facility. There are plans to add 10 more facilities in the next six months. This means a commensurate increase in staff, although it will be incremental and not immediate. There are 10 IT staff at headquarters to handle the needs of the entire organization. This staff will grow more slowly as they follow the growth of the rest of the company. Loan servicing has a staff of 65 whose responsibilities range from customer service to portfolio management to investor relations.

1. When creating OUs that allow different groups within the company to administer their own resources, you create a:
   a. centralized model
   b. distributed model
   c. combination model
   d. All of the above
   e. None of the above

2. Currently, the branches connect to the network through a VPN to update their regional offices with the orders they place for inspections, appraisals, and so on with local vendors. Given the expansion plans, this is adequate.
   a. True
   b. False

3. How do you determine the viability of the current network design?
   a. Analyze the current infrastructure.
   b. Look at the growth plans.
   c. Analyze network usage patterns.
   d. All of the above
   e. Answers a and c

4. Which of these items help to manage site implementation? (Choose all that apply.)
   a. Replication traffic
   b. Site-aware applications
   c. File replication service
   d. Logon traffic

5. What is the geographic scope(s) of this company? (Choose all that apply.)
   a. Regional
   b. National
   c. International
   d. Subsidiary
   e. Branch office

1.2 Analyze company processes: information flow, communication flow, service and product life cycles, and decision making processes

INFORMATION FLOW • COMMUNICATION FLOW • CYCLES • DECISION MAKING PROCESSES

UNDERSTANDING THE OBJECTIVE

Understanding how an organization makes decisions, communicates within itself and to customers, and the life cycles of its internal and external products is critical to properly designing AD. Remember, much of the structure of AD is for the network administrator. It is also important to review the company's policies and procedures to help determine this information.

WHAT YOU REALLY NEED TO KNOW

◆ In most cases, information flows from the top of the organizational structure down to the lower levels. On these lower levels, information may also flow laterally between departments. The flow of information in each organization can help determine who should have authority over whom. This information can be factored into your OU design for use with the Delegation of Authority Wizard.

◆ Like information flow, communication often flows from the top down. Communication flow is the human interaction between individuals in the company. However, there also tends to be a lot more communication upstream and between departments. Communication flow also includes communication with organizations and individuals outside the company, such as suppliers and customers. The communication flow may also affect the information flow, so it is important to understand both.

◆ Product life cycles usually begin with an idea, approval to pursue it, development, deployment, marketing, sales, support, and so on. Understanding a company's design, development, sales, support, and so on can lead to a better AD design. OUs can be designed by department, location, or product, and this information should be factored into the OU design.

◆ Decision making deals with how decisions are made, including who makes the decisions (individuals or groups), what information they need to make those decisions, how many are involved in making the decisions, at what level different types of decisions get made, and so on.

OBJECTIVES ON THE JOB

Information and communication flows are two keys to the success of any firm, and they become increasingly important as the company grows. Setting up the internal physical and software mechanisms to accommodate growth in information is the point of working with data dictionaries and schema to create stability and trust. IT is an essential part of the company's success as it verifies that information flows to the proper source and ensures the data's integrity.

PRACTICE TEST QUESTIONS

A tremendous amount of information flows in, through, and out of Coast Mortgage. First is the influx of new applicant information. This begins a series of events that culminates in the closing of the loan. Within the organization, many people are involved in the processing of this loan. Coast also has many investments, which frequently take a long time to mature and show positive cash flow. Management examines market conditions daily (and sometimes hourly) and makes fund-pricing decisions, effectively determining the return of an investment. Uninterrupted access to a constant stream of data is essential to the success of this activity. Without this information, inaccurate decisions are possible, which could result in faulty decisions and the loss of a considerable sum of money. The IT group is central to the success of this activity. Network reliability is considered a given by management and staff. Any interruption, even for 30 seconds, is considered unacceptable.

1. When deciding what action to take on any given project, what kind of documentation is necessary to make an informed decision? (Choose all that apply.)
    a. Risk assessments
    b. Troubleshooting information
    c. Optimization targets
    d. Growth assessments

2. The Customer Service Department operates around the clock, seven days a week. How should you schedule network maintenance to minimize interruptions?
    a. Schedule network maintenance in the early hours of the morning when few people call in.
    b. Use network redundancies to avoid any interruption.
    c. Place a note on the customer service Web page announcing the planned outage.
    d. The outage will be short enough to not cause any significant problems.

3. How should you delegate administrative authority to the decision makers?
    a. Assign the permissions to the administrative user object.
    b. Assign permissions at the domain level.
    c. Assign permissions at the OU level.
    d. Assign permissions to individual objects.
    e. Assign everyone domain administration rights.

4. Given that upper management needs access to most of the data in the company, it would be wise to delegate administrative authority to them at the domain level.
    a. True
    b. False

1.3 Analyze the existing and planned organizational structures: management model; company organization; vendor, partner, and customer relationships; and acquisition plans

BUSINESS MODELS • CENTRALIZED • DECENTRALIZED • AUTHORITY STRUCTURE

UNDERSTANDING THE OBJECTIVE

Properly designing AD for a company requires that the designer understand how the company is structured, its management model, its relationships with outside parties (customers, suppliers, and partners), and any plans the company has for acquisitions and/or divestitures. Windows 2000 is designed to easily scale from the smallest to the largest company.

WHAT YOU REALLY NEED TO KNOW

◆ Most companies' management models (sometimes also called business models) can be classified as centralized or decentralized, depending on the degree of central control and decentralized authority. Generally, the company's management model can be translated fairly easily into an OU design and/or a domain/tree/forest design. Centralized IT offers greater control and standardization throughout the network, at the cost of reduced flexibility. Decentralized IT offers greater flexibility to meet changing needs, at the cost of more heterogeneity, which increases the TCO at each location.

◆ Company organization refers to the authority structure within a company. There are two general models: hierarchical (triangle-shaped with multiple levels between top management and workers) and flat (with few, if any, levels between top management and workers).

◆ Outside relationships such as suppliers, distributors, and consumers are an organization's links to other companies. There may also be links for training, accounting, distribution, and so on. When considering the degree to which you wish to share resources with partners and suppliers, consider the degree of trust between the two companies, network connectivity issues, and security. These factors should be considered before, during, and after the relationship exists. These customers and partners generally do not need access to the company's network infrastructure, other than Web, FTP, and e-mail. The primary consideration is whether these services will be available to everyone or whether there will be an authentication mechanism for authorized customers to access these resources.

◆ When evaluating acquisition and divestiture plans, it is important to consider whether the networks will work together or be completely separated for the spinoff. This includes security issues, OS integration issues, training issues, and data flow issues.

OBJECTIVES ON THE JOB

All of these issues are critical to the proper design of AD. Although all require careful thought, be especially careful with acquisition and divestiture plans because Windows 2000 is designed to work with only one forest at a time.

PRACTICE TEST QUESTIONS

A new regional inspection company, Inspections Now!, comes calling, and management feels that this new firm has the ability to provide inspections in a more timely and cost-effective manner than the current suppliers. However, they are not ready to abandon any current relationships with vendors. A trial period is established, and, if all goes well, Inspection Now!'s position is assured. All of a sudden, Sales, Marketing, Accounting, IT, and Customer Service have a new entity with whom to deal. New personal relationships need to be established. Accounting needs to add a wealth of entries to the ledger, Sales and Marketing have additional items to market and price lists to prepare, and IT gets to integrate the entire process. IT will provide Inspections Now! with limited access to the information they need (as they do with all partners), such as dates and locations to be inspected.

1. The domain needs restructuring to accommodate the addition of Inspection Now!.
    a. True
    b. False

2. The global catalog will be modified with the addition of Inspection Now!'s access to Coast's resources.
    a. True
    b. False

3. How many OUs need to be added to provide Inspection Now! access to resources?
    a. One
    b. Three
    c. Four
    d. None

4. Inspection Now! wants to be able to connect to Coast's network to check the status of orders for inspections. What method will best accommodate this request?
    a. A direct connection to your network
    b. A VPN
    c. A dial-up connection
    d. All of the above

5. How does the addition of Inspection Now! as a vendor affect the schema?
    a. There is no effect.
    b. A new object within the schema is necessary.
    c. The data dictionary requires a new definition.
    d. A new log on scenario is needed.

1.4 Analyze factors that influence company strategies: identify company priorities, projected growth and strategy, relevant laws and regulations, the company's tolerance for risk, and the total cost of operations

PRIORITIES • TCO • FEDERAL, STATE, AND LOCAL • RISK TOLERANCE

UNDERSTANDING THE OBJECTIVE

What is the company's purpose? Why does it exist? Focusing on priorities helps a company direct its attention to the matters that make it succeed. Laws and regulations can impact the priorities, as can growth. TCO relates to the cost of the IT Department and all things related to IT. Risk tolerance relates to how much risk a company is willing to assume and how much they are willing to spend on mitigation and recovery policies.

WHAT YOU REALLY NEED TO KNOW

- ◆ A company's priorities help guide the company on everything it does. It guides decisions large and small and should be understood to bring all of the other details discussed in this section into focus.

- ◆ When considering growth, consider the following: personnel, infrastructure, and resources necessary to support all employees, disaster recovery plans, and so on.

- ◆ Laws and regulations at the federal, state, and local levels can all have a large impact on how a company conducts business. Consider varying restrictions on encryption, digital signatures, and security (such as C2), for example. Do laws require that data be kept private or published to the public?

- ◆ TCO relates to the cost of IT at all levels, including hardware, software, and data, as well as help desk, administration, and other personnel. The value of each component needs to be determined on a per-user or per-seat basis, as well as a total for the organization. What is the current value of each asset? What is the replacement cost of each? Also, consider the value of training each new staff member.

- ◆ Risk tolerance is simply the willingness of the company to gamble on the loss of one or more of the following: customers, security, personnel, data, equipment, and so on.

- ◆ A risk assessment should include the following: a list of risks, the probability of each occurring, and the severity of each risk (including both the scope and potential cost).

- ◆ Mitigation plans should be developed for each risk listed to reduce the probability of it occurring and contingency plans if it does occur. These plans should be part of the recovery plan. The idea is to simply reduce the chance of each risk occurring, and if it does, to minimize the costs.

OBJECTIVES ON THE JOB

The risk assessment should include nearly anything imaginable, including problems with AD, hardware, software, power outages, floods, winds, hurricanes, human intervention or inattention, and so on. Remember that human threats can come from both outside and inside the company and both must be carefully planned for and guarded against.

PRACTICE TEST QUESTIONS

Coast Mortgage must evaluate the offer of a community in another state in which to relocate its operations. The distance is great and local culture quite different from their current situation. Supposedly, the regulatory environment is far less restrictive, with fewer taxes and a less complex government infrastructure. The task is to find out if this is really the case and if there is any justification to the move. The company is considering growing into that state as an alternative to moving there, as well as considering maintaining a base of operations in both states.

1. Planning for growth requires many considerations. A new domain is one of them.
    a. True
    b. False

2. What is the potential effect of an interstate move on the IT Department? (Choose all that apply.)
    a. A redesign of the network
    b Acquisition of additional equipment
    c. Addition of new staff
    d. New regulatory concerns

3. What would the redesigned IT Department need to do?
    a. Accommodate a new operating system.
    b. Restructure permissions settings.
    c. Establish a new schema.
    d. Redefine the data dictionary.
    e. None of the above
    f. All of the above

4. When examining network design priorities, which are most important? (Choose all that apply.)
    a. The projected topology
    b. Equipment expense
    c. Access by the general staff
    d. None of the above

5. Which of the following should be included in the document outlining the rationale for or against the move? (Choose all that apply.)
    a. Disaster recovery plans for the transition period
    b. Disaster recovery plans for the new location
    c. Risk assessment
    d. TCO analysis for the hardware in the new location
    e. Mitigation plans for potential issues that may arise

1.5 Analyze the structure of IT management: type of administration, funding model, outsourcing, decision making process, and change management process

CENTRALIZED/DECENTRALIZED • FUNDING • CHANGE MANAGEMENT

UNDERSTANDING THE OBJECTIVE

The administrative model for a company's IT Department determines, to a large degree, how AD is designed. Different models can radically alter the design.

WHAT YOU REALLY NEED TO KNOW

◆ The funding model relates to how the IT Department gets the money for ongoing operations, upgrades, and so on, and can be either a general company budget or a portion of a department's budget. If IT is funded generally, it is often easier to set policies and design AD; whereas when money comes from each department, they often distrust others and want competing designs with differing amounts of security. AD is flexible and can accommodate most desires, but all competing interests must have their input into the design for the final product to be viable.

◆ Outsourcing refers to turning some or all of IT's responsibilities to an outside form. Key issues to be aware of are: security breaches due to the contractor's access to internal data, how emergencies and outages are handled, and the time it takes for off-site staff to get onsite to solve a problem.

◆ Change management refers to how changes are handled, such as upgrading or relocating workstations, granting Internet access, assigning IP addresses, and configuring a user's PC for telecommuting. What paperwork is required? To whom does it go? Who makes the decision on the change? Who implements it?

◆ Besides outsourcing IT, there are three basic administration models: centralized IT, centralized IT with decentralized management, and decentralized IT.

◆ In the centralized IT model, all IT work happens at a central location. This is most common in smaller organizations and in those that are very control-oriented.

◆ With the centralized IT with decentralized management model, a core group manages the "big picture" but leaves the day-to-day operations and decisions to those in the field. This is most often seen in larger organizations with many locations.

◆ The decentralized IT model takes all administrative control and spreads it out among regional, divisional, or other boundaries. There is no central IT group, so initiatives between groups require a lot of communication between them and/or software and services that let the various networks communicate with each other. This is seen most often in very large organizations in which different countries have different, independent authority over their own resources and in small companies that are growing rapidly.

OBJECTIVES ON THE JOB

The administrative model is the most important single factor in the design of AD.

PRACTICE TEST QUESTIONS

1. **What is the IT model used at Coast Mortgage?**
   a. Centralized IT
   b. Centralized IT with decentralized management
   c. Decentralized IT
   d. Outsourced IT

2. **A small flower distribution business recognizes the need for computers, but they do not have a lot of money or expertise in managing them. What is the best IT model for this situation?**
   a. Centralized IT
   b. Centralized IT with decentralized management
   c. Decentralized IT
   d. Outsourced IT

3. **A large, international company is having trouble maintaining control over its computing assets. Currently, administration takes place at each location. To increase efficiency and control over the network while reducing expenditures, the company is looking at alternatives. What is the best model(s) to achieve these goals? (Choose all that apply.)**
   a. Centralized IT
   b. Centralized IT with decentralized management
   c. Decentralized IT
   d. Outsourced IT

4. **The same company is very concerned about being able to respond quickly to changing market conditions to remain competitive. What is the best model to achieve these goals?**
   a. Centralized IT
   b. Centralized IT with decentralized management
   c. Decentralized IT
   d. Outsourced IT

5. **As companies grow and mature over time, the needs of the organization change, and structure often is added where there was little, if any. The policies and procedures that need to be followed to set up a new server should be documented in the:**
   a. Risk assessment
   b. Mitigation plan
   c. Change management document
   d. Help desk documentation

Section 2

Analyzing Technical Requirements

ABC Electric Supply

ABC Electric Supply is a multi-national provider of electrical components and design services for control systems integration. The company headquarters is located in York, PA. Approximately 3000 workers at this location engage in a variety of activities including engineering design, drafting, integration, component manufacturing, and company management, including HR, Payroll, Accounting, and IT. There are a total of 37 geographic locations that have anywhere from 15 to 500 employees. The Accounting and HR Departments each have their own file servers and manage them locally. The IT Department is responsible for all other computer resources. The company is divided into four divisions: Asian Manufacturing, European Sales, South American (SA) Sales, and North American (NA) Operations. The total number of worldwide employees for ABC Electric is 26,000.

The company recognizes the need to move forward with upgrading their computers from Windows 95, 98, and NT to Windows 2000. The need is evident on two fronts. First, the engineers designing the control systems are finding that customers want to use Windows 2000 for security reasons. Also, many of the companies that sell control integration software are upgrading their products to run under Windows 2000, and customers want the new features provided by the latest software releases.
A second issue plaguing the company is that the Accounting Department wants to implement a new version of their accounting software package that has been upgraded to run under SQL server. The older version runs under FoxPro and does not integrate well with the NT operating system installed on the accounting server. The accounting database has failed several times in the last few months, which has resulted in delays in issuing payroll and client billing. The manager of the Accounting Department thinks a fault-tolerant database design would resolve some of these problems.

ABC Electric is experiencing a period of high growth that is projected to continue for the foreseeable future. Approximately two new locations are being added each year, and the most rapid growth is now in the SA Sales division. Existing communications between sites range from T1 to DSL to 56 K dial-on-demand connections.

Due to the rapid rate of growth, the IT Department is frequently overwhelmed with the volume of support calls. In addition to providing support for technicians installing equipment and applications at the new locations, the increase in the number of users makes it difficult to answer all the support calls in a timely fashion. Support requests include problems accessing e-mail, application failures, and problems finding the correct printer to send jobs. In addition, users sometimes change their desktop settings or cause desktop failures by installing software from the Internet.

Although ABC Electric has Internet connectivity, not all segments of the network use TCP/IP. Some Windows 95 clients still use NWLink as their primary protocol, and frequently the Windows 95 users have difficulty accessing documents stored on NT Workstation PCs. The IT Department wants to standardize on TCP/IP in the future, but many applications require NetBIOS support. Although there is one WINS server, the network administrators are not confident that it works reliably because there are often garbled entries in the WINS database. The IT Department wants to spend more time troubleshooting problems on the servers and less time reconfiguring user desktops and installing applications.

The Accounting Department wants to be able to implement more electronic transactions including electronic payments to suppliers, electronic quarterly tax deposits to the IRS, and direct deposit to employees. However, the implementation of these new business strategies should not disrupt the day-to-day business of ABC Electric.

Because much of the business of ABC Electric Supply revolves around process control in manufacturing facilities, technicians and engineers in the Control Systems Design Department spend a lot of time out of town, installing and monitoring new installations. Some of their customers are large food processors and manufacturing facilities that generate millions of dollars of product each day. Any new equipment installation must be closely monitored to ensure that it does not interrupt the production lines. The technicians and engineers want ABC Electric to update its remote access capabilities to make it possible to establish VPN connections to customer plants for remote monitoring purposes. Many of them have DSL or cable modem connections at home and also want to be able to connect to their offices at ABC Electric in order to work from home part time.

Another ongoing problem is file sharing between the drafting technicians and the engineers. The CAD drawings for a project are initially created on the user desktop and then manually copied to the file servers. Often, it is months before the project is completed and the files are copied up to the server. If multiple users need to access the drawings at the same time, file shares are created at the PCs which have only 10 Mbps network cards rather than from the server which has a 100 Mbps network card and fast access SCSI hard drives. In addition, the users rarely back up their hard disks. The manager of the Engineering Department wants to have the files saved on the file server automatically, so all project files are backed up when the primary file server is backed up, and to make it easier to share access.
The manager of the Engineering Department is responsible for all the drawings generated by both the engineers and the drafting technicians until project completion. Because the information in the drawings is usually proprietary to the client, he wants complex passwords to be utilized when accessing these resources, even though the majority of the company does not deal with sensitive data.

Interviews with Company Employees

CEO - The stock price of ABC Electric Supply has been relatively stable given current market conditions. This is because we have consistently met our growth targets. However, to continue to remain at this level and to give our investors the increases in returns they expect, we must continue to stay competitive. In this market, technology must enhance the ability of the company to compete; it cannot be an end unto itself. Networks have become entirely too costly to maintain, and we need to find a way to reduce the TCO of the desktops by making desktop management more efficient. I expect the upgrade to Windows 2000 to improve my company's position in the marketplace by reducing my overall network support costs.

I also hope this will improve our chances of landing some large contracts by being an early adopter of new technology. Many control systems integrators are much larger than we are, so we have to compete by emphasizing our technological innovation. Also, our solutions need to fit smoothly into the overall network of the plants where we install our products. The larger organizations especially like to standardize their hardware and software. After looking at Microsoft's numbers for how many companies have already moved to Windows 2000 and the projections for those who are planning to upgrade within the next year, I realize we cannot hesitate with this upgrade, or we will be left behind in the dust.

IT Manager - We need a product like Windows 2000. If we can implement all the "Follow Me" features, it will make the work of our technicians much easier. Right now, unless they use laptop computers with all the applications installed locally, it is almost impossible for them to access all the specialized software needed to troubleshoot problems at remote sites. We tried using images to create the desktops, but there are so many customized software packages required, especially because we have offices in a lot of different countries. At least Windows 2000 makes it easier to provide language and dialect support.

As the network has grown, so has my staff. Right now, everyone tries to learn how to do everything—hardware, software, and networking—but at the rate technology is changing, it makes it impossible to keep the entire staff up-to-date. It would be beneficial to change to a strategy of specialization, or at least be able to design the network so that I could assign specific kinds of tasks to specific people.

It is kind of exciting to have the opportunity to install such a new product, but I worry whether it will solve all our problems. I want an environment that is easy to centrally manage so I can cut down on some of my travel costs and use it for technology reinvestment.

Accounting Manager - It wasn't so long ago that our network was just one server. Now, we have servers everywhere. It's hard to keep up with the pace of growth in this company, but it's necessary to keep the shareholders happy. I just purchased our new accounting software two years ago, and it's already out of date. I can't properly protect the data files, and now that we have this big initiative to get connected to the Internet, I worry about someone getting access to our confidential data. We have information about customers, products, and suppliers in our database, and that information is valuable.

The accounting database has been inaccessible on two different occasions. Each time, it cost us a deadline. It always seems to fail when we are trying to produce the most work. Once, we missed our payroll deadline and had to overnight payroll checks all over the world. That was costly downtime. We need a system that is reliable and can handle the large processing jobs like publishing yearly financial reports while running the payroll job at the same time. I am expecting Windows 2000 and SQL 2000 to solve some of these difficult problems for us.

Also, I want my staff to be able to occasionally work from home. We have people taking days off from work just waiting for furniture to be delivered. I want all the permanent employees in the Accounting Department to be able to connect to the accounting server across a secure connection and continue to do their work from home. Everything they need is online, and many employees already have a cable modem or DSL service. Also, they get fewer interruptions from home.

LAN Administrator - The network has become very complicated, very quickly. I started here just a few years ago, and since that time we have gained 50 new servers. It would not be such a problem if we did not have so many different domains. We have just one account domain, but there is a separate resource domain for accounting, engineering, and marketing, just at the headquarters. Many of the other locations have separate domains as well. We must have 20 different domains. Just maintaining all those trust relationships is difficult.

We also need to be familiar with all the software that we install at client sites, so we can help the engineers troubleshoot problems when they install servers at the client networks. The servers we install for clients are used to control and monitor entire assembly lines, and the software needs to be configured perfectly or a problem could go unnoticed. Any little problem in an assembly line could result in damaged product as the output. That is very costly to our customers.

It would be helpful to have an operating system that makes the network servers and the desktops easier to manage. I want to be able to remotely install the desktop operating system. I heard Windows 2000 could do that. I would like to test it in our lab, and see how well it works. It could be a big time saver.

Company Characteristics:
Budgeted Hardware/Software Expenditures for Current Year:
6 Dual Processor Pentium III servers, with RAID subsystems
3 Single Processor Pentium III servers
500 Pentium class workstations
3 Ethernet switches
2 Cisco 4500 routers
Windows 2000 Advanced Server for all existing servers

Number of Users per Site:
York, PA - 3287
Seattle - 466
Denver - 327
London - 488
Frankfurt - 35
Amsterdam - 116
Santiago - 17
San Paulo - 48
Jakarta - 456
Singapore - 485
Manila - 376
All other branch offices <25

Design Requirements:
Create an AD infrastructure that allows ABC Electric to continue to grow at its current rate without requiring an upgrade to the AD infrastructure for at least four years. Use AD to solve the technical support issues that result from the way the desktops are managed today. Include solutions in the design to solve problems with file sharing and remote access on the company network.

The design should stay within the budget constraints of ABC Electric and provide fault tolerance wherever it would substantially improve business operations. The design must be able to be managed without increasing the existing IT support staff. The stockholders of ABC Electric want the company to alleviate the need to hire additional staff by becoming more productive and using technology to improve business processes.

Identify areas that need network infrastructure upgrades to support the desired AD infrastructure. Use the existing infrastructure wherever possible. Suggest the most cost-effective solutions. For example, replace long-distance, dial-in solutions with VPNs across the Internet.

Security is a major concern in this design. However, security has costs in terms of bandwidth and performance. Identify areas of the network that require high, medium, and low security. Use Group Policies to balance security and performance.

Evaluate the way the company is currently using information. Suggest solutions that enhance access to information while improving the overall manageability of the network. Ensure that all network data is adequately protected while still being available as needed.

Try to keep the design of AD as simple as possible while still fulfilling the requirements of the organization. The goal is elegant simplicity.

ABC Electric Supply, Inc.
Organizational Chart

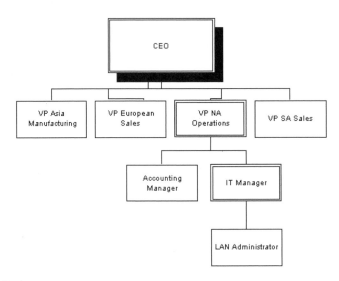

Figure 2-1

2.1.1 Evaluate the company's existing and planned technical environment: Analyze company size and user and resource distribution

GEOGRAPHICAL LOCATIONS • RESOURCE DISTRIBUTION

UNDERSTANDING THE OBJECTIVE

The company size and how users are organized into departments help to determine the AD design. If users are separated from the resources needed to perform their jobs, AD can make those resources appear local to the user, even if they are geographically separated.

WHAT YOU REALLY NEED TO KNOW

- ◆ Determine the number of geographic locations involved. The greater the number of locations, the more likely that users are separated from the information they require.

- ◆ Gather information about the user community from surveys completed by business unit managers. Understanding how the business operates is essential to designing a good AD structure.

- ◆ Define resources required for specific user groups. This can differ for each department.

- ◆ Obtain an organizational chart. This explains the relationships between internal company organizations and helps you determine how the network is currently administered. If there is a large IT Department, the company network is most likely managed centrally.

- ◆ Interview the IT Department and gather information about the existing information resources. This helps identify potential problems in the current IT infrastructure that may need improvement. Any situations that represent a single point of failure may point to problems that can be resolved in the new AD environment.

- ◆ AD can handle a virtually unlimited number of user and computer objects. The best designs, however, organize these objects to improve user access to resources, limit network traffic, and improve administrative control.

- ◆ Analyze how users access and make use of resources available on the network. In a campus environment, users may regularly utilize printers in other buildings. In a retail organization, in which storefronts are located in different cities, this is less likely.

- ◆ Applications that must be available to all users in the organization must be identified. These applications can be made available via domain or site-level group policies.

- ◆ Identify resources that only need to be available locally. The Engineering Department may have the only users that need access to a D-size drawing plotter.

OBJECTIVES ON THE JOB

Some departments may have unusual requirements for the way information is stored or accessed. Security may be a high priority for some departments but not for others. Ask users questions about the perceived complexity of accessing network resources. This can provide you with clues as to how to improve business processes while developing a network design.

PRACTICE TEST QUESTIONS

1. **Which document assists in determining the relationships between internal organizations?**
   a. Network diagram
   b. IT infrastructure diagram
   c. Organizational chart
   d. HR Database

2. **What is the best way to gather information about the way the company operates?**
   a. Organizational chart
   b. User surveys
   c. Network diagram
   d. Requirements document

3. **When developing an AD design, what goals should be satisfied? (Choose all that apply.)**
   a. Improve user access to resources.
   b. Increase the network bandwidth.
   c. Limit AD-related network traffic.
   d. Improve administrative control.

4. **How will reviewing the access to existing IT resources improve the AD design?**
   a. Eliminate single points of failure.
   b. Increase network bandwidth.
   c. Improve workgroup interaction.
   d. Determine language requirements.

5. **Why would it be important in an AD design to identify application needs of user groups?**
   a. To improve application deployment via group policies
   b. To ensure adequate network bandwidth for the application
   c. To improve network administration for the application
   d. To ensure user needs are met

2.1.2 Evaluate the company's existing and planned technical environment: Assess the available connectivity between the geographic location or worksites and remote sites

VPN • DSL • CABLE MODEMS • ISDN • REMOTE SITES

UNDERSTANDING THE OBJECTIVE

More and more networks are stretching across geographic boundaries that would not have been imagined even three years ago. Much of this globalization is built upon the considerable capabilities of the Internet and is driven by Web-based application development. Today's network operating systems include features like routing, remote access, and VPN services designed to satisfy our need to communicate with all our business partners.

WHAT YOU REALLY NEED TO KNOW

◆ Identify the geographical locations that will be directly connected in this design. Plan to have fast (512K or greater) communication links between all AD components. Geographic separation should be transparent to the user community.

◆ Obtain copies of all network documentation. This should include maps of the cable plant that specify existing LAN and WAN connections and the speed of these connections. AD uses these connections to replicate data.

◆ Determine all new locations that will be opened over the next two years. Interview company planners to determine what type of activities will be carried out at these new locations. In many cases, there may need to be a DNS or an AD component at these new locations.

◆ Gather information about the communication technologies that are available in each region. Different WAN services are available in different geographic areas. DSL, cable modems, and ISDN all have distance specifications that require the user to be within a particular range from where the service is offered. In addition, newer services like DSL require specialized equipment that some smaller telephone companies cannot provide if the population density does not warrant it.

◆ Choose telecommunication providers that can serve as many of your locations as possible.

OBJECTIVES ON THE JOB

Connectivity is the greatest concern in a network that spans large geographic areas. Often, e-mail is the only reliable and reasonable method of communication between employees who work in distant offices located in different time zones. LAN connections are easiest to manage because the company owns the resources and is responsible for maintenance and upgrades. WAN links are more difficult because you must rely on outside companies to provide the resources to create long-distance communication solutions.

PRACTICE TEST QUESTIONS

1. **You have been hired by ABC Electric Supply to design their AD. After analyzing the information contained in their proposal request, you develop your solution. What domain structure will you recommend for implementation at ABC Electric?**
   a. Multiple forest, multiple domains
   b. Single forest, multiple domains
   c. Single forest, single domain, no OUs
   d. Single forest, single domain, multiple OUs

2. **ABC Electric wants to design an AD infrastructure that allows users in all locations with more than 50 users to authenticate locally. What is the minimum number of domain controllers that are required?**
   a. Eight
   b. 11
   c. 16
   d. 18

3. **ABC Electric Supply has a domain that spans three continents. If the NA Operations Division has domain controllers in York, Seattle, and Denver, what is the minimum number of connections you would recommend between these cities to ensure constant communications access between the locations?**
   a. One
   b. Two
   c. Three
   d. Six

4. **What is the minimum number of DNS servers ABC Electric needs to support AD?**
   a. One
   b. Two
   c. Six
   d. Eight

5. **Some of the branch offices do not have dedicated WAN links for AD. How can ABC Electric accommodate user logons at these locations?**
   a. Create a separate forest.
   b. Create a separate domain with a dial-up link that synchronizes AD after hours.
   c. Install a dial-on-demand router to service AD requests.
   d. Create a separate OU.

2.1.3 Evaluate the company's existing and planned technical environment: Assess the net available bandwidth

NET AVAILABLE BANDWIDTH • ACTIVE DIRECTORY SIZER • NETWORK MONITOR

UNDERSTANDING THE OBJECTIVE

The net available bandwidth is the amount of bandwidth that remains after calculating the current usage of network bandwidth. This includes e-mail and other network applications, such as distributed DB servers and intranet Web servers. AD can add significant traffic to your network if you make changes to the AD database. Bandwidth is also consumed by DC replication and user authentication.

WHAT YOU REALLY NEED TO KNOW

- ◆ Determine how much of the existing bandwidth is being utilized. Network Monitor is a tool available in both NT and Windows 2000 that allows you to log usage across a network segment.

- ◆ Interview the managers of all the major departments to determine if there are any application development projects underway that may require additional network bandwidth. Use a benchmarking tool to forecast bandwidth usage for new network applications that have not yet been fully deployed.

- ◆ Decide whether all users will connect to the network via AD. This is a determining factor in the decision of where to locate AD domain controllers. Use the AD Sizer tool to determine how many sites, domain controllers, and Global Catalog servers are needed to support AD.

- ◆ Intersite replication via RPCs is significantly more efficient than the same traffic over SMTP. SMTP generates approximately 2.5 times the amount of traffic of RPC, even with compression.

- ◆ Calculate the amount of bandwidth needed to support AD operations by estimating how many objects, attributes, and changes will be made to AD. Most AD traffic is not compressed (intra-site), and this increases bandwidth requirements.

OBJECTIVES ON THE JOB

IT workers who manage the WAN should stay current with new technology because vendors offer new bandwidth solutions every day. Remote access has also become a necessity, and additional WAN resources will be required to satisfy users' desires to work when and where they want. Choose ISPs with the broadest range of services possible. Gather as much information as possible about the number of objects and attributes you expect to have in AD and how they will be distributed—whether in one domain or several. Microsoft recommends a single domain architecture for most environments.

PRACTICE TEST QUESTIONS

1. **What types of network changes result in AD traffic? (Choose all that apply.)**
   a. Password changes
   b. Creation of new users
   c. Creation of new sites
   d. Employee address changes

2. **The T1 link between the NA Operations and European Divisions is 70 percent utilized. What is the best way to control inter-site replication traffic between servers in the same domain?**
   a. Create a site link between NA and Europe using SMTP.
   b. Create a site link between NA and Europe using RPCs.
   c. Create a site link between NA and Europe using RPCs replication interval = 90 minutes.
   d. Create a site link between NA and Europe using SMTP replication interval = 45 minutes.

3. **What is the minimum number of domain controllers that is required if all users authenticate locally?**
   a. 11
   b. 37
   c. 39
   d. 41

4. **Global Catalog servers assist users in the authentication process by storing the membership of Universal Groups. On this network, what percentage of AD traffic will Global Catalog servers generate?**
   a. 10%
   b. 25%
   c. 50%
   d. 0%

5. **What is a key factor that determines the amount of traffic generated during user logon authentication?**
   a. LDAP queries for a domain controller
   b. DNS queries for a list of domain controllers
   c. Group policy processing
   d. DHCP queries for IP configuration information

OBJECTIVES

2.1.4 Evaluate the company's existing and planned technical environment: Analyze performance requirements

PERFORMANCE REQUIREMENTS

UNDERSTANDING THE OBJECTIVE

AD is the feature of Windows 2000 Server that provides domain services. The primary tasks that AD performs are user logon authentication and replication of the AD database. These important tasks can be affected by bandwidth availability, group policy object processing, and server hardware.

WHAT YOU REALLY NEED TO KNOW

- ◆ Group policies are applied at multiple levels within the AD structure. The total number of group policy objects that apply to a specific computer/user combination affects the length of time needed for logon processing. If possible, limit the number of GPOs that need to be processed at logon time to three.

- ◆ Use the AD Sizer tool to design the AD structure. The AD Sizer tool determines the CPU and disk specifications required to support your AD implementation. The more information you provide, the better results you achieve.

- ◆ AD relies on the network for transport services. Inadequate bandwidth resources may result in perceived performance degradation of AD services even if the server has been properly specified. Providing users local access to resources can enhance performance. Consider putting domain controllers at sites with large user populations.

- ◆ AD is a network application that competes for resource access with other applications in your environment. If an existing application already consumes a high percentage of CPU, disk, or network resources, assign additional resources that are dedicated to AD.

- ◆ Server downtime equates to a reduction in performance statistics. AD has built-in fault tolerance capabilities. Because all AD domain controllers are peer, adding domain controllers improves performance statistics by providing alternate authentication and LDAP query locations to users.

- ◆ Mobile users may encounter slow WAN links when accessing the network remotely. GPO processing can be configured to test for slow WAN links and process policies differently over different network connections. For example, folder redirection, script processing, and software installation can all be restricted over slow WAN links.

OBJECTIVES ON THE JOB

AD services require greater bandwidth, CPU processing, and disk and memory resources than NT domains. Evaluate hardware resources and network infrastructure to ensure that AD will not strain the existing environment and plan the necessary upgrades.

PRACTICE TEST QUESTIONS

1. **Group policy is applied at multiple levels of the AD structure. What is the best way to ensure that GPO processing does not negatively affect the perceived performance of the network?**
   a. Apply GPOs at the container closest to the user.
   b. Apply no more than three levels of GPOs.
   c. Apply GPOs at the site level.
   d. Apply GPOs at the domain level.

2. **How does the number of AD objects affect the design requirements of AD? (Choose all that apply.)**
   a. The number and type of objects determine the amount of disk space required.
   b. The number of objects determines how many sites should be established.
   c. The number of objects determines how many domains will be created.
   d. The number of objects can affect the time it takes to replicate across the network.

3. **User authentication is a critical operation in the network. The length of time it takes to log on to the network often influences users' perception of network performance. What can be done to optimize user logon authentication? (Choose all that apply.)**
   a. Position domain controllers close to large user populations.
   b. Apply as few GPOs as possible.
   c. Provide adequate bandwidth to support authentication for remote users.
   d. Create more OUs.

4. **The HR Department is planning to implement a newly distributed Web-based application that allows employees to query their personnel file. Because this information is of such a sensitive nature, the HR application developers have been planning to use IPSec to configure the Web servers to require security. Because IPSec increases bandwidth utilization, the network administrators want to estimate how much traffic this application will add to the network. What is the best way to determine this?**
   a. Use Network Monitor to capture packets flowing between the client and the servers.
   b. Have the developers use MSDN to create custom objects and counters that are used in System Monitor to track bytes sent across the network.
   c. Use Task Manager.
   d. Use the System Monitor Process object to track I/O statistics.

2.1.5 Evaluate the company's existing and planned technical environment: Analyze data and system access patterns

DATA AND SYSTEM ACCESS PATTERNS • SHARED FOLDERS • DFS • OPERATIONS MASTERS

UNDERSTANDING THE OBJECTIVE

Networks are designed to improve employee efficiency and reduce process redundancies by creating a framework that allows information to flow freely throughout an organization. AD can enhance this framework by allowing network administrators to organize resources so that they are visible to the users who need them.

WHAT YOU REALLY NEED TO KNOW

◆ Shared folders is a new feature in AD that exposes information stored in the file system. Windows 2000 operating systems, and any workstation that has the Directory Services client installed, can issue an LDAP search based upon keywords defined by the LAN administrator to describe the information represented in the shared folder.

◆ The Distributed File System has been enhanced in Windows 2000 to take advantage of fault tolerance features provided by AD services that enable information to be automatically replicated to servers throughout the network.

◆ AD uses Operations Masters to control important AD functions. For example, the RID Master controls the allocations of SIDs that are assigned to each new object created in the domain. By default, all these roles are assigned to the first domain controller installed in the forest and domain.

◆ By default, all DCs are installed in the site Default-first-site-name. Workstations are automatically assigned site membership based upon IP address. If no domain controllers for the user's domain exist in the local site, it takes longer to complete the user authentication process. However, if domain controllers for a domain exist in two different sites, it increases latency associated with AD replication. Increasing the performance of user authentication can cause a corresponding decrease in replication performance because these two parameters have an inverse relationship.

OBJECTIVES ON THE JOB

Performance is in the eye of the beholder, and what constitutes an improvement in performance for one network characteristic can result in decreasing performance for another characteristic. Define which network characteristics are most important: fast logon authentication, low replication latency, increased net available bandwidth, or fast application access.

PRACTICE TEST QUESTIONS

1. **The IT Department wants to provide users with the most accurate AD data possible. Which network characteristic is most important?**
   a. Replication latency
   b. Authentication processing
   c. Net available bandwidth
   d. Security

2. **The Finance Department is creating a Request for Proposal to solicit bids for a new accounting software package. The manager of the Finance Department wants as much input as possible to ensure that all current and future requirements are satisfied by the new application. A new Windows 2000 AD network has just been installed. How can the network administrator help users find the correct folder location for the proposal input without having to change users' desktop configurations?**
   a. Create a shared folder named Proposal. Map a drive on the Finance users' desktops.
   b. Create a shared folder named Proposal. Map a drive in the Login Script for the Finance Department.
   c. Create a shared folder named Proposal in the Finance OU. Create keywords to enhance LDAP search capabilities. Publish this folder in OU=Finance.
   d. Create a DFS link called Proposal.

3. **ABC Electric Supply has installed a new Windows 2000 AD network. This morning, the first domain controller installed in the network was taken offline to perform some required maintenance. The IT Department has also scheduled an NT domain upgrade this morning. How can the AD structure be configured to provide access to all the data required to import the NT domain objects into AD?**
   a. Move the role of Schema Master, RID Master, and Domain Naming Master to a different domain controller.
   b. Move the role of RID Master to a different domain controller.
   c. Move the role of Infrastructure Master to a different domain controller.
   d. Move the role of PDC Emulator, RID Master, and Infrastructure Master to another domain controller.

4. **The Accounting Department wants to install SQL Server 2000 and upgrade the existing accounting database server to Windows 2000 Advanced Server. What feature of Advanced Server could ensure continuous access to the data?**
   a. Clustering
   b. AD replication
   c. Publishing a shared folder in AD
   d. File Replication Services

OBJECTIVES

2.1.6 Evaluate the company's existing and planned technical environment: Analyze network roles and responsibilities

NETWORK ROLES AND RESPONSIBILITIES • DELEGATION OF AUTHORITY

UNDERSTANDING THE OBJECTIVE

The primary goal of the AD infrastructure design is to facilitate network administration. Organizations have different ways of managing networks that range from centralized to completely distributed, but are usually some combination of the two. Political concerns may also be reflected in the network management model, although the capabilities of AD can satisfy most requirements for local management of resource security.

WHAT YOU REALLY NEED TO KNOW

- ◆ The AD hierarchy can be designed based upon geographic locations, company organization, or departmental functions. The most important factor in deciding which type of design to use is whether it can function properly even in the face of business restructuring.

- ◆ Organizations with large numbers of resource domains should be able to reduce the total number of domains by using OUs. Administrative independence can be maintained by using delegation of authority to distribute control of some network resources to local OU administrators.

- ◆ Authority can be delegated at either the object or the task level, enabling IT managers to obtain the best combination of centralized control and distributed task management.

- ◆ Authority may be delegated at the site, domain, or OU level. Be sure to consider the automatic inheritance features of AD when delegating authority.

- ◆ Delegation of authority makes it possible to reduce the number of domain administrators. Fewer domain administrators mean that network managers can be assigned more limited resource access.

- ◆ Secondary logon is a new capability in Windows 2000 that allows a user to log on with a user ID that has access levels specific to a task. This allows LAN administrators to be logged on with a user ID that exposes fewer security risks, most of the time. When a task that requires administrative privileges is about to be invoked, the administrator starts the job with the user account that has elevated privileges.

OBJECTIVES ON THE JOB

Today's corporate environment is very dynamic, and the AD design should withstand reorganizations, acquisitions of new business entities, and mergers with industry partners. The goal of delegating administrative authority should be to reduce the TCO for the network overall. Administrative tools in AD have been designed to facilitate this goal.

PRACTICE TEST QUESTIONS

1. The Accounting Department is concerned about maintaining the confidentiality of the company's financial data. In the current economic environment, the slightest drop in corporate earnings easily frightens stockholders. ABC Electric wants to maintain strict control over all communications to the public regarding financial results. What is the best way to allow the Accounting Department to maintain control of their data?
   a. Create a separate forest.
   b. Create a separate tree called Accounting.
   c. Create a separate Accounting domain.
   d. Create a separate OU called Accounting, and delegate authority to the accounting manager.

2. Most of the LAN Administrators in the IT Department are members of the Domain Admins group. The IT manager is concerned about LAN administrators logging on to the network and leaving their desks without logging off. How can the LAN administrators change their work habits and reduce the risks of exposing the network to security breaches?
   a. Use a screen saver password.
   b. Log on with a user account that has limited resource access, and use Run as with their domain Admins accounts to perform specific administrative tasks that require elevated privileges.
   c. Set a group policy to automatically log off members of the domain administrator group after a period of keyboard inactivity.
   d. Log on with their Domain Administrator account, and use Secondary logons for other activities.

3. The IT Department staff has been averaging 15 hours of overtime each week. In addition to being costly for the department, many employees are unwilling to continue working under these conditions, and the department's turnover rate is twice that of other departments. Administrators complain that much of the work they do, such as resetting passwords, does not require their specialized skills. How can the IT Department resolve some of these issues?
   a. Create container administrators at the OU level.
   b. Hire more LAN administrators.
   c. Delegate the authority to reset passwords and update certain AD object properties to users at the OU level.
   d. Hire less skilled workers.

4. Resetting passwords is an example of what type of delegation?
   a. Object-level delegation
   b. Task-level delegation
   c. OU-level delegation
   d. Network-level delegation

2.1.7 Evaluate the company's existing and planned technical environment: Analyze security considerations

SECURITY • GPO • KERBEROS

UNDERSTANDING THE OBJECTIVE

Security has become an overriding concern for many network administrators in recent years. This is largely due to the increase in external connections to partners, customers, and suppliers. One of the most common ways of creating these external connections is through the Internet, which is the largest WAN in the world. By default, communication across the Internet is insecure, and network administrators need to design a security infrastructure to protect vital company assets.

WHAT YOU REALLY NEED TO KNOW

◆ AD can help you enforce your security rules by applying security as part of a GPO.

◆ Design an IPSec security policy for network communications. This policy defines how packets are protected as they pass across different parts of your network. IPSec can also provide protection for mobile users making remote access connections.

◆ Analyze account policy restrictions, and determine if policies need to be applied at the domain or OU level. Global user accounts obtain their account policy from the domain GPO. Local user accounts can obtain account policies from an OU level GPO where the computer object exists. There is only one domain account policy.

◆ Determine whether changes are needed for the default Kerberos Policy. This policy can only be changed at the domain level, which means it persists throughout all OUs in the domain.

◆ Local policies can be enforced throughout the domain using group policies. If a workstation or server is created in a Windows 2000 domain, its local policy is overridden by the local policy settings of the GPOs created in the domain or OU of which it is a member.

◆ Determine how to handle data access by users outside your Windows 2000 domain. If Web-based applications will be used, explore firewall solutions that complement the security of your internal network.

OBJECTIVES ON THE JOB

The Internet was designed to foster open computing and resource sharing. Within your local LAN, create a security environment that satisfies corporate objectives for providing information access to appropriate individuals while repelling undesirable access to private or confidential data. This can be achieved through a combination of data encryption, secure authentication, and file system security.

PRACTICE TEST QUESTIONS

1. **Outside salespeople frequently visit ABC Electric Supply to market new products and demonstrate new applications that ABC Electric can use in their integration projects. The salespeople are frequently in areas that contain company PCs. How can the IT manager ensure that outside salespeople do not gain access to the network? (Choose all that apply.)**
   a. Create a domain-wide account policy that requires user passwords.
   b. Create an OU GPO that requires user passwords and sets an intruder detection policy.
   c. Include intruder detection settings in a domain-wide account policy.
   d. Assign screen saver passwords on the desktop.

2. **The engineering manager used the local security policy tool on several Windows 2000 Professional PCs to set intruder detection limits in an account policy. The domain and OU GPOs do not contain intruder detection limits. What will be the effective security settings on the Windows 2000 Professional PCs?**
   a. The domain GPO account policy overrides the local policy.
   b. The OU account policy settings will take precedence.
   c. The intruder detection limits of the local policy will be in effect.
   d. No account policies will be applied.

3. **A small group of users is working on a joint control integration project for Hershey Foods. The manager of the Drafting Department at ABC Electric Supply wants to provide local access to the W2K workstations of these users for file sharing. However, the information on these PCs describes the client's proprietary process, and the drafting manager wants secure passwords to be used on the local user accounts. The domain account policy does not require complex passwords. How can group policy be used to ensure that users connecting to these PCs using local accounts will utilize secure passwords?**
   a. Define a domain account policy to require complex passwords in the domain where the user objects exist.
   b. Define an account policy requiring complex passwords in the OU where the user objects exist.
   c. Define a domain account policy to require complex passwords in the domain where the computer objects exist.
   d. Define an account policy requiring complex passwords in the Drafting OU where the computer objects exist.

4. **How can Kerberos policies protect Web-accessible information?**
   a. Disable anonymous access.
   b. Enable Integrated Windows authentication.
   c. Enable Basic authentication.
   d. Enable Digest authentication.

2.2.1 Analyze the impact of Active Directory on the existing and planned technical environment: Assess existing systems and applications

EXISTING SYSTEMS AND APPLICATIONS • FILE SECURITY REQUIREMENTS • GPO

UNDERSTANDING THE OBJECTIVE

Windows 2000 can have a profound impact on a company's network environment. New features in AD allow control of local group membership and Registry settings, and allow administrators to protect important system files throughout the enterprise. This enables organizations to reduce the TCO of managing large, complex networks.

WHAT YOU REALLY NEED TO KNOW

◆ GPOs can be created to centrally manage group membership. For example, manage the membership of the Backup Operators group throughout the entire domain by creating GPOs that enforce the membership list. This strategy allows the IT Department to leverage scarce technical resources by eliminating the necessity of administering security at each desktop PC.

◆ Analyze file security requirements for important read-only folders that appear on PCs. Create a GPO that automatically protects these files from being deleted or changed. This can significantly reduce calls to the Help Desk by preventing users from accidentally removing files during disk cleanup operations. Users may not be aware of the function of many of the files on their PCs and may delete any that appear unfamiliar.

◆ Protect the Registry on PCs in the enterprise by restricting access to appropriate technical and administrative personnel. Create a GPO to enforce the security restrictions necessary to create a stable PC configuration.

◆ Be aware that multiple levels of GPOs can be assigned to the same resource. Analyze how GPOs will be applied to eliminate redundant policy settings. Plan to test all GPOs in an offline environment or testing lab so as not to cause undue distractions during business hours.

◆ Users will continue to need access to non-Windows resources. Plan a strategy for providing access to these resources that leverages the capabilities of AD. For example, remote users may not need to have group policies applied to Windows 2000 PCs located in their home offices.

OBJECTIVES ON THE JOB

Existing systems that previously required separate, private networks can now be safely integrated with the rest of the company infrastructure due to the reliable application of GPOs that enforce mandatory security requirements. This increases the productivity of users on the private network as accessibility to other corporate resources is made available.

PRACTICE TEST QUESTIONS

1. **A user from the Accounting OU calls the Help Desk and explains that they accidentally deleted the Explorer.exe file from their Windows 2000 Professional PC. What is the best way for the Help Desk to deal with this situation?**
   a. Restore the file from a backup of the user's PC.
   b. Reinstall Windows 2000 Professional.
   c. Create a group policy object that prevents the user from deleting files from the \Winnt directory.
   d. Do nothing. The file will automatically be restored from the dllcache directory.

2. **Users in the Manufacturing Department need access to an application on a NetWare server. The manager in the Manufacturing Department wants to ensure that all users have access to this application without having to map a drive from the Tools menu in Explorer. What is the best way to ensure that a persistent mapping will always be created on the desktop of all the users?**
   a. Log on as Administrator on the PCs. Create a drive mapping for the NetWare application. Copy the Administrator profile to the default user profile.
   b. Create a login script with a persistent mapping to the NetWare application. Associate the login script with a GPO, and link the GPO to the Manufacturing OU.
   c. Log on as Administrator. Put the NetWare application in the Startup folder. Copy the startup folder to All Users.
   d. Make all users supervisors on the NetWare server, and create a startup script that automatically launches the application when the PC is booted.

3. **A domain-level GPO limits resource access to the \Winnt directory. The OU administrator of the Engineering Department has created another GPO that limits access to the \System32 subdirectory. Analyze the effect of these policies.**
   a. The OU-level GPO is unnecessary.
   b. The domain-level GPO will be ignored.
   c. The domain-level GPO and OU-level GPO will be applied.
   d. GPO policy will not be applied due to conflicts between domain and OU GPOs.

2.2.2 Analyze the impact of Active Directory on the existing and planned technical environment: Identify existing and planned upgrades and rollouts

UPGRADES AND ROLLOUTS

UNDERSTANDING THE OBJECTIVE

Organizations have great flexibility in deciding how to implement the upgrade to Windows 2000. Whether companies decide to upgrade client desktops first, or servers and domain controllers, any move toward the new operating system yields benefits. Many enterprises have opted to upgrade the client PCs first, in order to have time to plan and test the AD implementation. This is a good choice because there are many decisions that need to be made about how AD best serves a particular organization.

WHAT YOU REALLY NEED TO KNOW

◆ Windows 2000 Professional workstations can smoothly integrate into a Windows NT domain environment. Although the workstations look first for a Kerberos KDC, they automatically search for an NT LAN Manager domain controller if a KDC does not respond.

◆ Windows 2000 AD DCs can support down-level operating systems. The AD DCs offer both Kerberos and NT LAN Manager authentication services to satisfy requests for multiple versions of SMB services.

◆ If the NT PDC is upgraded to AD, BDCs continue to participate by providing authentication services. This is made possible through NT LM replication services. This service is no longer provided once an AD domain has changed from mixed to native mode.

◆ With AD in place, new administrative services are available to help move users quickly into the Windows 2000 environment. For example, the RIS provides a way to quickly upgrade many down-level operating systems to Windows 2000 Professional. Multiple RIS servers can be installed to provide load balancing, especially during the initial implementation period. These servers can then take on other responsibilities in the Windows 2000 environment.

◆ If fully configured desktops are what you need, use RIS to create RIPrep images for each type of client desktop configuration required. This gets your users up and running as quickly as possible with the applications they need.

OBJECTIVES ON THE JOB

Examine the reason why your organization is moving toward Windows 2000, and use that as a guide to determine whether to upgrade client PCs, or servers and domain controllers, first. Remember, the sooner AD is installed in your network, the sooner you can move to a native mode environment and take full advantage of AD's features.

PRACTICE TEST QUESTIONS

1. **How many Windows NT domain controllers can be supported in a native mode AD domain?**
   - a. An unlimited number
   - b. Zero
   - c. No more than five
   - d. Less than 10

2. **ABC Electric Supply currently has a mixed mode AD domain. Which domain controller authenticates the Windows 98 PCs? (Choose all that apply.)**
   - a. A Windows 2000 PDC
   - b. A Windows NT PDC
   - c. A Windows 2000 BDC
   - d. A Windows NT BDC

3. **ABC Electric Supply is opening a new facility in Malaysia. Due to some delays in equipment delivery, the project is behind schedule and management wants to bring the network online as quickly as possible. How can AD reduce the time needed to implement the new network?**
   - a. Use RIS to install Windows 2000 Professional. Install applications on each PC.
   - b. Ship all PCs to York, PA. Unpack PCs, install Windows 2000 using RIS, repackage PCs, and ship to the new site.
   - c. Build separate images for each type of hardware configuration. Push images to PCs.
   - d. Create RIPrep images on multiple RIS servers.

4. **ABC Electric has an existing 24 X 7 network of Windows 95 and 98 PCs. AD has been installed. What is the most efficient way to deploy Windows 2000 to the PCs without impacting the bandwidth to existing applications?**
   - a. Use one RIS server to install Windows 2000 on PCs.
   - b. Use multiple RIS servers, on different segments, to load balance network bandwidth usage.
   - c. Build separate images for each type of hardware configuration. Push images to PCs.
   - d. Perform installations during the evening hours.

5. **ABC Electric has a network of Windows 2000 domain controllers and Windows NT Workstation, Windows 98, and Windows 95 PCs. When can ABC Electric change from mixed to native mode?**
   - a. When all Windows NT workstations are upgraded to Windows 2000
   - b. When all Windows 98 and Windows 95 PCs are upgraded to Windows 2000
   - c. When all client PCs are Windows 2000
   - d. The PCs do not need to be upgraded. Switch to native mode now.

2.2.3 Analyze the impact of Active Directory on the existing and planned technical environment: Analyze technical support structure

TECHNICAL SUPPORT STRUCTURE • AD

UNDERSTANDING THE OBJECTIVE

Companies approach network support in a variety of ways. In some companies, LAN administration is casual. PC gurus pop up in each department, volunteering to help others with their network problems. In many companies, however, technical support has evolved into a multi-layered model that seeks to categorize problems based upon severity and automatically assigns the appropriate support technician to resolve the issue.

WHAT YOU REALLY NEED TO KNOW

◆ Categorize network activities to determine which tasks should be handled by experienced network technicians and which tasks can be handled by knowledgeable users within a particular OU. For example, resetting passwords is a task that can easily be handled by someone within a department rather than requiring a network administrator.

◆ Design AD based upon how the network will be managed. For example, if you want to decentralize some of your network support, create OUs along departmental or divisional lines so that authority for the container can be easily delegated. This might include tasks such as creating user and computer objects, servicing printers, or resetting passwords.

◆ Existing NT networks can easily be rolled up into a much smaller Windows 2000 model by refining NT resource domains as Windows 2000 OUs. Container administrators can be given responsibility for important server resources by including those server objects in the OU.

◆ Examine the features of group policies to see if GPOs can be used to reduce the number of support calls that come in to the Help Desk. One of the features of the software installation and maintenance technology is resilience, the ability of the application to be self-mending. If a user accidentally deletes a file necessary to the proper operation of the application, group policies can correct that action.

OBJECTIVES ON THE JOB

How your company approaches technical support and network administration is a key issue in determining the appropriate AD model. The decentralized department approach requires many more containers to ensure that network administration decisions made in one department do not affect users in other departments. A more formal, centralized approach results in a roll up of the AD structure because fewer boundaries are needed to protect special interests.

PRACTICE TEST QUESTIONS

1. **ABC Electric Supply has a centralized IT Department at the company's headquarters in York, PA. The company needs to decide how it will leverage its existing technical resources to support the new AD infrastructure. The Accounting, Manufacturing, and Engineering departments all have at least one person who is knowledgeable about the network. Match the following tasks to the group that should perform those tasks: LAN Administrators or OU Administrators.**
   a. Create new domains.
   b. Reset users' passwords.
   c. Change document printing order.
   d. Add new object attributes to the AD schema.
   e. Install new network cards in PCs.
   f. Create new user objects.

2. **Currently, the Accounting Department has its own NT resource domain because the information in the accounting database is sensitive and company confidential. The manager of the Accounting Department wants to ensure that unauthorized users do not gain access to this information. What is the best way to design AD to accommodate this concern?**
   a. Make the Accounting Department its own OU.
   b. Make the Accounting Department its own domain.
   c. Store the accounting servers in a locked room.
   d. Move the accounting servers to the IT server room.

3. **ABC Electric Supply has one account domain and five NT resource domains. What is the most likely AD structure to evolve from this network design?**
   a. One forest, five domains
   b. One domain, five OUs
   c. One forest, one domain, one tree, five OUs
   d. Five forests

4. **The accounting manager wants a copy of the timesheet application to be installed on all workstations in the domain. How can AD facilitate this?**
   a. Create a GPO in Computer Configuration that assigns an application link to Accounting OU.
   b. Create a GPO in User Configuration that assigns an application link to Accounting OU.
   c. Create a GPO in User Configuration that publishes an application link to Accounting OU.
   d. Create a GPO in Computer Configuration that assigns an application link to the domain.

2.2.4 Analyze the impact of Active Directory on the existing and planned technical environment: Analyze existing and planned network and system management

NETWORK AND SYSTEM MANAGEMENT

UNDERSTANDING THE OBJECTIVE

System downtime is an IT manager's nightmare. At best, system outages can be embarrassing to a highly skilled staff of technical professionals. At worst, outages can cost the company money. How much money the outages cost depends on how long the outage lasts and the scope of its effects. As a result, most network training courses include at least one chapter on how to be proactive in identifying potential problems in the network. The Windows 2000 OS can help network managers avoid the helpless feeling that erupts when downtime occurs.

WHAT YOU REALLY NEED TO KNOW

- ◆ Monitor important system resources. This allows network administrators to be proactive in dealing with the network environment.

- ◆ Plan a system of notification that alerts members of the technical staff about sudden changes in important OS characteristics. At a minimum, an alert should be generated when certain sustained memory, disk, or CPU resources change by 10 percent or more.

- ◆ Utilize the Windows 2000 Resource Kit applications and the utilities that can be installed from the Support Tools directory on the Windows 2000 CD-ROM to view information about the health of directory replication.

- ◆ DNS is a required component in a Windows 2000 domain. If a DNS server is unavailable, users are unable to locate a domain controller to service their authentication request. Check the DNS log for a list of recent unsuccessful DNS update events.

- ◆ To allow technical staff to concentrate on servicing network infrastructure problems, plan on delegating authority for specific tasks or delegating the management responsibility to create, manage, and delete network objects, such as users, groups, and PCs.

OBJECTIVES ON THE JOB

Windows 2000 has several new features to improve the network administrator's chances of discovering a potential problem before it causes system downtime. There are three new event logs: DNS Server, File Replication System, and Directory Service. Active monitoring of these logs alerts technicians to pending conditions that may cause future failures. For example, the AD log issues an NTDS KCC entry if it cannot contact a replication partner after a certain number of tries.

PRACTICE TEST QUESTIONS

1. **Users at one of the sites in the Philippines are complaining that it takes a long time to log on. The network is configured with a local domain controller and DNS server at the site. What is an easy way for a network technician in York, PA to determine if there is a problem with the domain controller at the users' site?**
    a. Use Network Monitor to monitor traffic passing to the onsite domain controller.
    b. Use the Replication Monitor tool to see if there is a problem with replication updates.
    c. Use the AD event log to see if there are any errors replicating to the on-site server.
    d. Monitor the Network Segment using the System Monitor tool.

2. **Users at the new Malaysia facility are unable to complete LDAP searches for AD objects. A check of the network management station indicates that the communications link between Malaysia and the Philippines is down. Why are users unable to complete LDAP searches?**
    a. The DNS server is located at the Philippines site.
    b. The WINS server is located at the Philippines site.
    c. The DHCP server is located at the Philippines site.
    d. The Kerberos service is not running.

3. **The IT Department wants to be able to query services on the Windows 2000 domain controllers from the SNMP management station. How is this configured in Windows 2000? (Choose all that apply.)**
    a. Administrative Tools, Computer Management, Services, Configure SNMP service
    b. Administrative Tools, Services, Configure SNMP service
    c. Right-click My Network Places, Properties
    d. Settings, Network and Dial-up connections, Properties

4. **Which tool is used to generate alerts about important system resources?**
    a. Performance Monitor
    b. Performance Logs and Alerts
    c. System Monitor ActiveX Control
    d. Microsoft Management Console

2.3.1 Analyze the business requirements for client computer desktop management: Analyze end-user work needs

END-USER WORK NEEDS

UNDERSTANDING THE OBJECTIVE

Network users should have an environment that makes accessing the network transparent. One of the ways to implement this is by creating persistent drive mappings. In addition, network access times should be reasonable. Remember that child containers inherit group policy settings. When designing the AD structure, use this inheritance to reduce the number of levels at which group policy settings need to be applied. AD should also be configured to deal with the multitude of venues users have for connecting to the network. Do not assume that these types of parameters are fixed.

WHAT YOU REALLY NEED TO KNOW

- ◆ Users need access to disk resources, but a few users can inadvertently drain the resource pool. Use group policy to manage disk quotas automatically. This reduces the TCO for the organization by allowing technicians to leverage their scarce time.

- ◆ Users need access to a variety of applications to perform their job duties. The greater the number of applications to be supported, the greater the amount of time required for help desk and technical support requests. Use AD to establish a good compromise between support costs and meeting user software requests.

- ◆ Implement group policy settings that take into account the type of connection the user is currently assigned. Some group policies, like software installation, can have a negative impact on authentication time. Make use of slow link detection settings by analyzing your communication options and defining what is considered slow in your enterprise. Security policy is always applied, even across a slow link.

- ◆ Be sure to consider the effect of policies on mobile users. If a user is likely to connect from multiple sites within the network, strive to provide a consistent interface and appropriate application support. Without the proper application accessibility, users are not productive, and company efficiency suffers. Remember, a primary goal of Windows 2000 is to reduce TCO. Improving worker efficiency accomplishes this.

OBJECTIVES ON THE JOB

When designing AD structure, consider how the application of group policy affects user logons. If you do not have SMS, consider using the Software Installation and Maintenance features of Windows 2000 to automate user access to applications. User access to applications should be independent of network location. Some users change their location frequently. The AD design should take this into account and define a structure that allows GPOs to be applied appropriately.

PRACTICE TEST QUESTIONS

1. **The network administrators at ABC Electric Supply frequently travel to different sites to implement new hardware and software installations or to perform troubleshooting tasks. How can the AD structure be designed to improve the technicians' access to utilities needed to perform their jobs?**
   a. Create a separate domain for the technicians.
   b. Create the technicians' user objects in a separate OU, and create a GPO to assign the required applications to their PCs.
   c. Create the technicians' user objects in a separate OU, and create a GPO that assigns the applications to the user objects.
   d. Create a separate domain for the technicians, and create a GPO that publishes the required applications to their PCs.

2. **Members of the Engineering Department at ABC Electric Supply frequently dial in from home to work on client projects. How can AD be designed to reduce the amount of time it takes the engineers to get connected from home?**
   a. Create an Engineering OU, and link a GPO that monitors the slow link detection settings.
   b. Create an Engineering OU, and link a GPO that detects whether they are connecting from the LAN or the WAN.
   c. Create an Engineering Domain, and link a GPO that monitors the slow link detection settings.
   d. Create an Engineering Domain, and link a GPO that detects whether they are connecting from the LAN or the WAN.

3. **Workers in the Manufacturing Department use the Internet to identify products that will improve their control integration process. One day last week, one of the workers downloaded a number of new applications along with sample implementation scenarios and product literature. Workers began to receive errors indicating that the server was out of disk space on the user volume. The file servers are in a Servers OU. Which of the following AD designs could potentially eliminate this problem?**
   a. Create a GPO in the domain that assigns disk quotas, and link it to the Manufacturing OU.
   b. Create a GPO in the Manufacturing OU that assigns disk quotas and enforces disk space limits.
   c. Create a GPO in the Domain Controllers OU that assigns disk quotas and enforces disk space limits.
   d. Create a GPO in the domain that assigns disk quotas and enforces disk space limits.

2.3.2 Analyze the business requirements for client computer desktop management: Identify technical support needs for end users

TECHNICAL SUPPORT NEEDS • GROUP POLICIES • INHERITANCE

UNDERSTANDING THE OBJECTIVE

The stated goal of the Windows 2000 OS is to reduce an organization's TCO. Because support costs have been identified as one of the more costly components of information systems, this should mean that Windows 2000 reduces the need to provide technical support to end users. Indeed, Microsoft has included a vast array of wizards in Windows 2000 that they term "Troubleshooters". These applets walk users through a series of technical questions aimed at pointing the user to a viable solution that eliminates the need to call a Help Desk.

WHAT YOU REALLY NEED TO KNOW

◆ Group policies can be used to simplify the application of client configuration information. However, there are numerous rules about how group policies are assigned. Awareness of the rules assists designers in planning a functional AD design.

◆ You cannot assign a software policy to a PC that is a domain controller. So, if you have PC technicians providing technical support to users, the software they use must be installed on a client desktop.

◆ You should use inheritance as much as possible to reduce the task of troubleshooting group policy. You can apply broad policies at higher levels in the AD infrastructure and allow the policies to flow down to lower-level OUs.

◆ It is important to avoid exceeding three GPOs for any single PC or user. Too many levels of GPOs make troubleshooting the effect of multiple policies more difficult.

◆ Restricted groups, system services, Registry, and file system policies can be used to control the default system operation.

OBJECTIVES ON THE JOB

Consider the way departments within the company use information resources. Some departments determine the number of geographic locations involved in this design. The greater the number of locations, the more likely it is that users are geographically separated from the information they require and may have unusual requirements for the way that information is stored or accessed. Security may be a high priority for some departments, but not for others. Ask users questions about the perceived complexity of accessing network resources. This can provide you with clues as to how to improve business processes while developing a network design.

PRACTICE TEST QUESTIONS

1. **ABC Electric wants to provide technical support at each geographic location that contains more than 150 users. How can the AD design support this goal?**
   a. Create a domain at each geographic location with more than 150 users.
   b. Create an OU at each geographic location with more than 150 users.
   c. Create a tree for each geographic location with more than 150 users.
   d. Create a site for each geographic location with more than 150 users.

2. **ABC Electric has a group of technical support technicians that services all the PCs in the SA Sales Division. The SA Sales Division will be an OU within the primary company domain. The technicians need access to software that allows them to test the physical components in the PCs. All technicians will log on to the primary company domain. How should the testing software be installed?**
   a. Apply a group policy to the SA Sales Division OU that assigns the software to the PCs.
   b. Apply a group policy to the SA Sales Division OU that assigns the software to the users.
   c. Apply a group policy to the domain controllers OU that assigns the software to the PCs.
   d. Create an OU for the technical support technicians, and create their user objects in this OU. Apply a group policy to the technical support OU that assigns the software to the users.

3. **ABC Electric has created an AD infrastructure that includes three levels of OUs. The first level is a geographic region, the second level is the strategic business units within that geographic region, and the third is for departments within the strategic business units. The IT Department wants everyone in the company to have access to an office suite for basic application availability. Where should the GPO be applied?**
   a. Apply at the GPO closest to the user so the local administrator has as much control as possible.
   b. Apply at the domain level so it can be inherited across sites.
   c. Apply at the geographic OU level, and allow it to be inherited by the lower-level OUs.
   d. Apply at the site level so it can be inherited across all domains.

4. **ABC Electric's IT Department wants someone within each departmental OU to be responsible for updating users' address and telephone information. What is the best way to assign that delegation of authority?**
   a. Create a new OU for attribute administrators.
   b. Create a security group of attribute administrators in the departmental OUs.
   c. Create a security group of attribute administrators in the geographic OUs.
   d. Create a security group of attribute administrators in the primary company domain. Assign the appropriate delegation rights.

2.3.3 Analyze the business requirements for client computer desktop management: Establish the required client computer environment

CLIENT COMPUTER ENVIRONMENT • OFFLINE FILES • ROAMING PROFILES • FOLDER REDIRECTION

UNDERSTANDING THE OBJECTIVE

Establishing a fixed desktop environment with Windows 2000 is easier than in previous versions of the Windows OS. Group policies, a feature of AD, promises to correct the flaws of System Policies under NT and add a number of new capabilities. Follow Me is the new configuration management strategy fostered by a series of complementary services in Windows 2000 that enable a user to have their desktop environment, application access, and file system available without regard to the log on location.

WHAT YOU REALLY NEED TO KNOW

♦ No more tattooing the Registry. Under Windows NT, when a system policy was created, it changed the Registry of the local PC and remained unless a system policy was created that changed those Registry locations. When a group policy is assigned, it typically modifies one of four Registry locations under HKEY_CURRENT_USER or HKEY_LOCAL_MACHINE. When a policy no longer applies to a user or PC, the Registry entries are automatically removed at the next group policy refresh time.

♦ By default, group policy changes are replicated between domain controllers in the same domain every five minutes. Policy updates to the clients occur approximately every 90 minutes.

♦ The Offline Files feature allows users to access their data whether they are logged on to the network or using a mobile computer offline. Once a file or set of files has been marked for offline usage, updates are automatically synchronized between the mobile computer and the network server where the data is also stored.

♦ Roaming Profiles is another feature of the Follow Me technology that redirects a user's profile information to a location on a network server specified by a LAN administrator. The profile is then available from any site in the enterprise that has a connection to the profile server.

♦ Folder Redirection pushes files normally stored on a user's local PC to a network server. Used in conjunction with Offline Files and Roaming Profiles, this can give a user complete access to all necessary network information from any location.

OBJECTIVES ON THE JOB

Consider the way departments within the company use information resources. Some departments may have unusual requirements for the way information is stored or accessed. Security may be a high priority for some departments, but not for others. Ask users questions about the perceived complexity of accessing network resources. This can provide you with clues as to how to improve business processes while developing a network design.

PRACTICE TEST QUESTIONS

1. **ABC Electric's Accounting Department has created a standard accounting desktop design that puts a corporate logo in the background, removes the Run command from the Start Menu, and assigns a standard accounting application to all PCs in the department. These changes are pushed using a group policy object. A user is promoted to the Human Resources Department as a manager. A technician for the Accounting Department has moved the user's PC to their new office. What must be done to remove the accounting application and correct the Registry for the policy changes affected by the GPO?**
   a. Nothing, the Registry is automatically updated.
   b. Move the computer object from the accounting OU to the HR OU.
   c. Move the user object from the accounting OU to the HR OU.
   d. Move both the computer and the user from the accounting OU to the HR OU.

2. **The Vice President of the Asian Manufacturing Division at ABC Electric is concerned about data integrity on the local PCs. The IT Department has created a GPO for the Asian Manufacturing Division to initiate Folder Redirection for the My Documents folder for all PCs. If the policy was ready for deployment at 1:00 p.m. and the next replication cycle is 1:30 p.m., how long will it take the GPO to be implemented?**
   a. 30 minutes for intra-site users, 30 minutes = scheduled interval for inter-site users
   b. 30 minutes
   c. The GPO will not be implemented.
   d. It depends on when the user logs on to the PC.

3. **A new technician has been hired by ABC Electric's IT Department to support the European Sales Division. The technician needs to test a PC at a remote location that has demand dial routing at night as the only connectivity. The technician starts a laptop computer that she uses when at remote sites and is surprised to find her PC hardware test software application available on the PC. What feature of Group Policy has made this application available even though the application is normally accessed from the network?**
   a. Offline Files
   b. Folder Redirection
   c. Roaming Profiles
   d. Local Profiles

4. **Managers within ABC Electric's strategic business units frequently visit remote sites for inspection and service provision. The managers use laptop computers at the sites and receive the same desktop configuration as when they are logged on from their regular offices. What feature of AD supports this?**
   a. Folder Redirection
   b. Offline Files
   c. Roaming Profiles
   d. Group policies

Section 3

Designing a Directory Service Architecture

CASE STUDY

Pharmco

Pharmco is a U.S.-based pharmaceutical corporation that has grown to have a worldwide presence. The company specializes in developing drugs for treating important health problems in North America, such as heart disease and some forms of cancer. The company is also involved in a number of joint projects with other organizations, such as the Centers for Disease Control, to develop products to combat some critical health issues that have evolved recently, such as AIDS and the Ebola virus.

The major company divisions include Research, Manufacturing, Distribution, and Operations. The Operations Division is geographically dispersed so that Pharmco can support local company facilities with the specific services required by a certain corporate location. Employee benefits vary from location to location based upon the prevailing cultural and economic norms for a given area.

Due to the globalization of world markets, Pharmco has been able to improve company productivity and shareholder returns by moving some of its manufacturing operations overseas. This has led to an increasingly diverse workforce that speaks 20 languages. Although most employees speak English, Pharmco has decided to configure its PC base to support both the predominant native language and English. Pharmco sees this as a way to foster company loyalty and hopes that this will enhance its reputation as a company that is sensitive to employee needs.

Pharmco has recently acquired a major subsidiary, Meredith Drugs, which has developed a series of drugs for the treatment of rare forms of cancer and certain types of diabetes. Meredith Drugs has an established reputation in the pharmaceutical industry and has a well-known identity on the Internet. This new subsidiary broadens the number of products that Pharmco can bring to the marketplace and makes available a body of cancer research and patents on cancer drugs that will bring Pharmco to the top of the industry for providing oncological medications.

Pharmco, Inc. has courted a major university to become a joint partner in genetic research. Pharmco plans on offering internship programs to a number of genetic engineering students at the university each year. The interns will be chosen based upon project proposals submitted to the various departments within the Research Division. Interns will be selected based upon how closely their area of research corresponds to targeted research initiatives that have been identified by Pharmco's Research Review Board. This partnership gives Pharmco access to some of the finest new talent in genetic engineering, and the internship program allows Pharmco to reduce some of their research costs because the interns will be compensated at a much lower rate than the full-time scientists conducting the same type of research.

Pharmco runs a number of clinical tests in which people suffering from certain forms of cancer or who have particular kinds of heart disease can be volunteered by their doctors to participate in clinical evaluations of new drug treatments. These programs are relatively low-cost to the patients and generally offer a much greater probability of attaining a positive outcome than the commercially available alternative. Doctors receive faxed copies of patient test results on a monthly basis, because there is little administrative support in the research units.

Pharmco is facing a number of challenges as it moves into the 21st century. First, aging computer technology is thwarting the ability of their talented engineering and scientific staff to work up the complex models required to develop drugs that can combat increasingly drug-resistant organisms. In addition, genetic research requires the most up-to-date hardware and very sophisticated software modeling programs to develop credible models of drug therapy and interaction. The IT Department has recommended replacing all the computers at several research facilities with high-end graphical workstations and re-deploying the existing PCs to less technologically aggressive portions of the company. The Manufacturing Division wants to move toward greater factory automation, and this means incorporating more computers into the production line. The factory floor operators in some of the non-U.S. facilities have little or no computer experience. This means the PCs that are deployed in these locations should be self-configuring and able to be remotely monitored and controlled by the IT Department. In addition, the software that is loaded on these PCs needs to be self-repairing in case an employee inadvertently deletes an important file. Managers and production line supervisors want the ability to log on to the company network and monitor the progress of the jobs controlled by the factory automation PCs so they can predict production statistics and be alerted to any work stoppages caused by equipment failure on the production line.

The doctors with patients in the clinical studies are dissatisfied with the delay in receiving information about the patients' medical progress. Many of the studies being conducted are treating aggressive forms of cancer. Patients who are non-responsive to a particular drug treatment may need to be re-evaluated and placed in another cancer treatment program. Doctors need to receive test results in a timely fashion in order to analyze the results and make appropriate decisions regarding patient therapy. The doctors are asking to make online connections to Pharmco's databases that contain the results of the clinical tests so they can stay apprised of the latest clinical information.

Many of the interns that will be involved in the research program at Pharmco are enrolled in advanced degree programs at Stevenson Institute of Technology. Each intern has been assigned a thesis advisor. The thesis advisors are faculty members who have some knowledge regarding the subject area of the thesis candidate. The thesis advisors at Stevenson need to have an evaluation of the intern submitted prior to the end of the school's term to form a basis for grading.

Stevenson expects to be conducting joint projects with Pharmco for the foreseeable future and wants to establish a mechanism for joint information exchange. Patents that are submitted as a result of the interns' contributions will be jointly shared by Stevenson, the intern, and Pharmco. This makes the relationship between Stevenson and Pharmco unique.

Interviews

Pharmco CEO - This is a very exciting time for the pharmaceutical industry. New genetic breakthroughs are occurring every day, and this leads to better opportunities for drug development. In addition, as our population ages, we are seeing a unique set of health issues present themselves and cry out for more creative and innovative solutions. At the same time, technologies, such as painless injections, represent a move toward kinder treatments and more consideration for the comfort of the patient. All of this opens the door to new research areas and creative solutions.

Although it is clear that the patient is and should be the primary concern, we need to remember that we also have a responsibility to our shareholders who require a reasonable return on their investment in order to continue to support the company's activities. If we neglect to provide the kind of returns that our shareholders expect, our competition will overwhelm us. Our mission should be to provide the most effective products we can while still maximizing shareholder returns.

Technology allows us to do the kind of advanced science that leads to the development of new drug patents. Without a sizable investment in technology, our scientists and researchers will be unable to decode the complex structures of our chemical makeup. We need to stay at the forefront of medical research to compete effectively and provide the kind of solutions that patients require. The growth of our company relies on applying technology effectively to decrease time to market. This is key to obtaining market share to establish a competitive advantage.

Doctor - It is very important to receive test results regarding a patient's condition in a timely fashion. The pattern of response that the patient develops each time they receive a new course of treatment can help to predict the ultimate success or failure of a treatment for a specific patient. In addition, patient outcomes can be affected by their state of mind. If a patient goes too long without a positive evaluation, it may negatively impact their response to future courses of treatment.

Many oncological treatments are detrimental to the overall health of the patients. Some treatments can seriously impair the function of vital organs and systems that are unrelated to the cancerous component. Patients involved in a clinical study that is not benefiting their condition should be allowed to withdraw to consider placement in a different clinical study or to re-evaluate their treatment options. Without timely access to the information gathered by the research scientists, as a doctor I am not able to provide my patient with the best level of care.

On the other hand, patient privacy is a serious matter and should be given the utmost consideration as we formulate a solution to this problem of information access. The data should not be inadvertently exposed to anyone not directly involved in the clinical study. Medical professionals other than the patient's doctors should get prior approval from the patient before accessing the records regarding the patient's condition. It is important that the data be secure even while the data access is occurring, just as it is when you connect to your financial institution.

Dean of Stevenson Institute of Technology - Our relationship with Pharmco is a unique opportunity to provide students with skills that can only be developed in a real-world situation. It is also an important way to increase the visibility of the school because important research patents provide access to publicity. The financial gains may also become important because we participate in equal shares in the rewards gained from patent royalties.

The main concern at the present moment is how we can improve communication between the staff at Stevenson and the researchers and company representatives at Pharmco. Internet mail is only a limited capability and relies on the generosity of a third party to provide information. Access to some of the information that is being developed in the lab could provide an excellent source for materials to include in future course offerings. The key is to be able to screen out the project-sensitive information and gain access to the purely academic topics, such as new research methodologies and laboratory procedures. Our network managers want to ensure that any communication link that is established between the two entities protects access to sensitive areas of our network as much as Pharmco's. This promises to be a subject of political debate as the project moves forward.

Pharmco IT Manager - The company is embarking on an ambitious plan to upgrade the workstations in key areas of the company. We need to plan the implementation carefully so as not to over-allocate our IT staff. If we can find a way to work more efficiently, we can optimize our IT resources. We are planning to use the group policy features of Active Directory (AD) to streamline the configuration of our desktop PCs and reduce calls to the IT Help Desk. This will free up resources for new installations and project implementation. Our IT Department has a hybrid structure in which some components of the network are managed centrally and some components are managed locally. The Help Desk is centrally managed, but we also have staff at some of the larger locations to deal with hardware and troubleshoot communication problems.

My concern is that we are expanding the scope of the network dramatically but will not be adding new personnel resources to manage the networks. We need to find a way to delegate some of the everyday administration of the network, like creating user objects and updating object properties to the business units. I understand there is a way to do this in the AD design.

I am also concerned about users working from home. I want to ensure that when the users connect to the network remotely, they are subject to a policy that protects data as it is coming across the remote network. The Internet is our preferred remote network because it reduces our telecommunication expenses. We want to eliminate all but two of our 800# lines connected to the remote access system and have most people connect to a local service provider and then VPN into the network.
The newest challenge that we will encounter in the months ahead is how to incorporate our latest business acquisition in this AD design and how to establish the appropriate relationship with our new University partner. We also need to address the concerns of the doctors who have patients involved in our clinical drug tests. We need to perform much more specific network configuration due, to the greater number of connections being made by individuals outside our organization.

Design Requirements:

Pharmco needs to upgrade its enterprise network from multiple Windows NT domains to a Windows 2000 domain structure. Create an AD design that accommodates the new subsidiary, Meredith Drugs, as well as their new educational and research partner, Stevenson Institute of Technology. Focus on a solution that allows users to exchange information as easily as possible without compromising existing Internet identities or information not directly related to partnering opportunities. Design a naming strategy that enables resources to be readily identified, even if users access the resources infrequently. The naming strategy needs to encompass all elements of the network, but the DNS naming structure is pivotal to providing a framework within which to create the AD domain structure.

DNS services are currently provided by a number of local ISPs, but the IT Department wants to deploy internal DNS servers to support AD. The IT Department wants to continue to have most DNS services handled by ISPs local to the largest sites but wants all users to be able to access the Internet for research and software updates, as well as to have a mechanism for partner knowledge exchange.
Clearly, some parts of the network need a high degree of security, but the network utilizes a large number of WAN links. We need to optimize traffic across the WAN links but have the ability to provide data and authentication security when and where it is needed.

A new level of remote access service is required to support the way workers perform their jobs. These remote access services need to be carefully configured to provide the best possible levels of security because the Internet will be our primary method of providing WAN connectivity. The remote access users should not compromise the integrity of data at the company's physical locations. The IT Department wants to continue to maintain its existing network administration model. Having some tasks centralized and others distributed has been a good working model and has allowed the IT Department to deploy sophisticated technology in geographical areas where the degree of technical knowledge does not exist.

The AD design should also include plans for the deployment of group policies and a determination of how AD schema changes can be accommodated in a network that has a geographical spread that encompasses the world. AD replication should not consume so much bandwidth that company business cannot be carried out in a timely fashion. In addition, this design should make clear any changes or upgrades that need to be made to the network infrastructure to reduce replication latency to one hour or less between sites with 1500 or more users. It is important to keep in mind that although information exchange is an important priority, Pharmco and Stevenson Institute of Technology are vastly different types of organizations and will have a need for different types of AD object classes and properties.

3.1.1 Design an Active Directory forest and domain structure: Design a forest and schema structure

FOREST • SCHEMA • GLOBAL CATALOG

UNDERSTANDING THE OBJECTIVE

After the AD design team has collected and analyzed all of the relevant data regarding the enterprise, the decision making process begins. The first decision that needs to be made regarding the AD design is whether to have a single forest or multiple forests. This is a key decision that all other design issues affect.

WHAT YOU REALLY NEED TO KNOW

- ◆ All domains in a single forest share a common configuration, schema, and global catalog.
- ◆ Sharing a global catalog means that users can easily search for objects across the entire forest. Users can only see objects for which they have read object permissions. If a user does not have read permissions for an AD object, it is not returned as a result in a search.
- ◆ Any change made to the schema in a forest is propagated throughout the entire forest. This means, if an additional attribute is added to the user object class, the attribute can be assigned to all user objects in the forest.
- ◆ The forest represents a group of organizations that have a need to share common objects and access resources easily. If organizations need to have different schema objects and attributes, they have to be in different forests.
- ◆ Companies or organizations that are completely different in their operation, business strategies, and functionality should be created as separate forests because the opportunity to share resources is very limited, and it is difficult to agree on a shared security scheme.
- ◆ Multiple forests have different spans of control. The two forests require separate administration and, therefore, higher overhead for the enterprise as a whole. Only create separate forests if the two organizations do not have significant interaction.
- ◆ Each forest has its own independent replication scheme, so domains in different forests do not share the same configuration or schema data. Changes made in one forest are not propagated to another forest.

OBJECTIVES ON THE JOB

Microsoft recommends single-forest and, if possible, single-domain designs, because this is the easiest design to implement and manage. Multiple forests do not share a common configuration, schema, or global catalog. This means that users in two different forests, performing the same search, achieve different search results. In other words, even if an object with the same name exists in each forest, it is an entirely different object.

PRACTICE TEST QUESTIONS

1. The IT Department at Pharmco, Inc. needs to decide whether to create a single forest or multiple forests. The managers in some divisions are wary of allowing the IT Department to create one all-encompassing forest and diluting what they consider to be an element of control. In addition, the recent agreements with Stevenson Institute of Technology have raised questions about how best to share data with other external entities. What types of criteria can help the department analysts make their decision? (Choose all that apply.)
   a. Boundaries for data and resource sharing
   b. Political alliances
   c. The type of network infrastructure
   d. Whether two businesses are closely aligned and share any form of management

2. Managers in the Research, Manufacturing, and Distribution Divisions currently have a number of resource domains as a way of independently managing their data and want assurances that they will have the same level of security and control when their NT domains become part of the forest. What information about AD can the design team use to answer the divisions' concerns?
   a. AD can be partitioned into domains that have independent administration.
   b. Domains have different sets of objects.
   c. A transitive trust relationship between the domains still requires administrators in the domain with the resource to assign permissions.
   d. All of the above

3. The Manufacturing Division uses specialized software to control their assembly line operations. The software, when upgraded to Windows 2000, creates its own objects in AD for managing the assembly line environment. When the new software is deployed, it needs to update the AD schema. If Pharmco uses a multi-domain model to implement AD, which domains will be affected when the schema is updated with the new object types?
   a. Manufacturing domain
   b. Manufacturing domain and forest root domain
   c. All domains
   d. None of the domains will be affected until they issue an apply schema command.

4. How does Pharmco's distributed geographical structure affect the number of forests?
   a. Geography has no effect on the number of forests.
   b. Pharmco needs different forests for each supported language.
   c. Pharmco needs multiple forests if T1 lines cannot be installed.
   d. Pharmco cannot create a domain that goes across multiple continents.

3.1.2 Design an Active Directory forest and domain structure: Design a domain structure

FOREST ROOT DOMAIN • REPLICATION

UNDERSTANDING THE OBJECTIVE

Domains create the security boundaries within a forest. Each area within a forest that requires separate security policies, such as password lengths, expiration intervals, or Kerberos policies, determines a new domain boundary. If the entire forest can use the same security policy and there is only one corporate identity shared by all organizations, then only one domain is required in the AD design.

WHAT YOU REALLY NEED TO KNOW

◆ Each domain has a separate Administrators local group and Domain Admins global group, so each domain is separately administered.

◆ The forest root domain has a special role within the forest and contains some special groups that do not appear in the other domains. The Schema Administrators and Enterprise Administrators groups only exist in the forest root domain. It is from these groups that the forest root domain receives its additional levels of administrative privileges.

◆ The forest root domain is the first domain in the forest and cannot be removed. If the forest root domain is deleted, the entire AD structure must be recreated. The name of the forest root domain is also the name of the forest.

◆ Information about objects created in the domain is only replicated to other domain controllers within the same domain. This makes a domain a unit of replication and is a way to partition AD.

◆ The number of domains in AD should be fewer than the number of domains under NT for a given organization. This is because Windows 2000 has the ability to delegate security for both AD object management and data management.

◆ Replication can consume significant bandwidth if the number of objects in the domain is high and there are frequent changes to object properties. All domain controllers within a domain participate in replication. So, if there is an area of the network that already has high bandwidth utilization, this may be an indication that another domain is needed to reduce replication-related data. Generally, this is a concern in areas of the network that are connected by relatively slow WAN links.

OBJECTIVES ON THE JOB

Under NT, the size of a domain was restricted to the size of the SAM database, which was 40 MB. This was equivalent to approximately 40,000 user objects. In Windows 2000, the maximum database size for AD is 70 TB, and each domain can hold 1 to 2 million objects. Therefore, the number of domains should be smaller in an AD environment.

PRACTICE TEST QUESTIONS

1. **What criteria does the Pharmco AD design need to consider when determining the number of domains? (Choose all that apply.)**
   a. Security
   b. Number of changes needing to be replicated between domain controllers in a domain
   c. Organizational chart
   d. HR Database

2. **How many domain local Administrators groups are there in a forest?**
   a. As many as the Enterprise Administrators create
   b. One for each resource administrator
   c. One for each domain
   d. One located in the forest root domain

3. **Pharmco has a number of Windows NT domains. The Operations Division includes the Human Resources Department and the Accounting Department. The Operations Division has a password policy that requires complex passwords and password expiration every 15 days. The Distribution Division has several NT domains, but all domains use eight character passwords and have password expirations set to every 90 days. The design team members from the Distribution Division do not want their users to have to change passwords every 15 days. What is the best solution for this problem?**
   a. Create a separate forest for the Distribution Division.
   b. Create a separate domain for the Distribution Division.
   c. Create a separate forest for the Operations Division.
   d. Create a separate domain for the Operations Division.

4. **Pharmco is organized into strategic business units that are independent profit centers. Pharmco utilizes a matrix management structure for some of the IT and accounting functions as a way of aligning the cost of providing services to the various business units. This means that users who are members of the IT and Accounting Departments need access to resources in two domains, their home domain and the strategic business unit they support. Where should the user's object be created?**
   a. In their home domains
   b. In the domain where the resources for the strategic business unit reside
   c. In both their home domain and the strategic business unit domain
   d. In the home domain, because the object will be replicated to the strategic business unit

3.1.3 Design an Active Directory forest and domain structure: Analyze and optimize trust relationships

TRANSITIVE • SHORTCUT • EXPLICIT

UNDERSTANDING THE OBJECTIVE

AD automatically creates transitive trust relationships between existing domains and new trees and domains that are added to the forest.

WHAT YOU REALLY NEED TO KNOW

- ◆ Windows 2000 uses transitive trust relationships to allow users to be assigned permission to forest objects without requiring extensive coordination between administrators in different domains.

- ◆ Data can only be shared between forests by creating NT style trust relationships, which are non-transitive and one-way.

- ◆ There are three different kinds of trust relationships in Windows 2000: transitive, explicit, and shortcut trusts. Each is used to solve a particular kind of resource sharing problem.

- ◆ Transitive trusts are the most common kind of trusts in Windows 2000. Transitive trust relationships are recreated automatically between parent and child domains. If domains are created three deep, the third-level child domain is able to access resources in the top-level parent domain because of the transitive nature of the trusts. (For instance, if A trusts B and B trusts C, then A automatically trusts C.)

- ◆ Shortcut trusts are used to create a direct authentication path between two child domains that might be three or more levels deep in a multiple domain, multiple tree forest. Rather than following a trust path that works its way up to the forest root domain and then down a different tree through several layers of parent domains, the child domains can create shortcut trusts that are transitive and shorten the authentication path that is normally followed when access to resources is requested between forests.

- ◆ Explicit trusts are trust relationships that are created between domains in two different forests. Normally, users in different forests are unable to access resources that exist in remote forests. Creating a one-way trust relationship allows users in one domain to access resources in another domain. To make all resources in both domains available to users in either domain, you need two one-way trust relationships.

OBJECTIVES ON THE JOB

Users gain access to resources in a Windows 2000 network using Kerberos service tickets. Every user is granted a ticket-granting ticket when they authenticate by the domain controller in their home domain. This ticket is used to ask for service tickets to access resources on a PC in the domain. To access resources in a different domain, a referral ticket is used to obtain a service ticket from a domain controller in a remote domain.

PRACTICE TEST QUESTIONS

1. **By default, what kinds of trust relationships will be created in the Pharmco forest?**
   - a. Transitive trusts
   - b. Shortcut trusts
   - c. Explicit trusts
   - d. One-way trusts

2. **Pharmco has decided to create a domain structure that encompasses two trees and three levels of domains in each tree. Users in the third-level child domain complain that it often takes a long time to open a file the first time, when accessing a file from the other tree. What causes this delay, and how could it be corrected?**
   - a. Users in the third-level domain must pass through multiple domain controllers in order to be granted a service ticket on the desired resource. The solution is to create an explicit trust to the other domain, so resources can be accessed more directly.
   - b. Users in the third-level domain must pass through multiple domain controllers to be granted a service ticket on the desired resource. The solution is to create a shortcut trust to the other domain, so resources can be accessed more directly.
   - c. Users in the third-level domain can directly access the other domain controller using transitive trusts, but the other domain cannot see the requesting domain's resources without being granted administrative privileges in the requesting domain.
   - d. It is not possible to access resources in a domain that is not immediately connected.

3. **Pharmco needs to be able to provide access to doctors who have patients participating in clinical drug trials for oncological drugs. However, Pharmco does not want to create a user account for the doctors. Most of the doctors' offices have small NT domains for patient records systems. What is the easiest way to give the doctors access to the Pharmco domain that contains the research servers for the clinical drug trials?**
   - a. Create a local account for the doctors in the domain where the servers reside.
   - b. Create a global account in the forest root domain, so the doctors have access to all data in the forest.
   - c. Set up a shortcut trust from the doctors' domains to the server domain.
   - d. Create an explicit trust from the server domain to the doctors' NT domains.

4. **Transitive trust relationships are used in Windows 2000 to facilitate the issuance of service tickets between domains that may not be directly connected either logically in the AD design or physically across the network.**
   - a. True
   - b. False

3.2.1 Design an Active Directory naming strategy: Establish the scope of the Active Directory

ACTIVE DIRECTORY FOREST • DOMAIN CONTROLLERS

UNDERSTANDING THE OBJECTIVE

Establishing the scope of AD means deciding which parts of an enterprise participate in an AD forest and how the participation is fostered. As long as a business entity is included somewhere in the AD forest, the users in that entity are able to fully participate in resource access. This assumes an underlying network infrastructure to facilitate data passing and authentication, even though some elements of an organization may only have access via demand-dial routing or other non-permanent connections.

WHAT YOU REALLY NEED TO KNOW

◆ For a specific part of the business enterprise to be included in the AD forest, there must be at least some form of inbound and outbound communication. If a site does not have reliable communication, it is not possible for it to participate in the AD forest. This is due to either authentication problems or replication problems.

◆ All domain controllers in a forest must be able to communicate on a regular schedule. That schedule may only be one time per week, but this is adequate to update a remote domain controller supporting only a few users.

◆ Microsoft's recommendation is that the AD design should result in a simple design, with one forest, and the fewest number of trees and domains possible.

◆ The goal of the AD design team should be to create a solution that improves business processes by removing barriers to resource sharing. This is always balanced by applying adequate ACLs to organizational resources.

◆ The scope of the AD forest should include all business elements that can potentially share resources. For this, you must rely on the data collected from each business unit. Often, users exchange data in informal ways, such as e-mail, removable media, or even print documentation.

OBJECTIVES ON THE JOB

Although Microsoft has made available recommendations about creating the AD infrastructure, many organizations may not be able to achieve the level of simplicity that is recommended by Microsoft engineers. In some cases, the structure may evolve more as a result of political posturing than as a result of the long hours of data collection and analysis completed by the AD design team. Still, even if the AD design has one or two more domains than necessary, the Windows 2000 operating system is rigorous enough to compensate.

PRACTICE TEST QUESTIONS

1. **The Research Division within Pharmco has lobbied to be allowed to create a separate forest. Members of the Marketing Department in the Operations Division often access information held in the servers in the Research Division to create advertisements for newly patented drugs. Should the AD design team give in to the Research Department's concerns about security and industrial espionage and create a separately managed forest?**
   a. No, because one of the tests for inclusion in a forest is the necessity to access resources on a regular basis.
   b. No, because then the other divisions will also want their own forests.
   c. Yes, because you can create explicit trusts across domains.
   d. Yes, because political concerns are an important element of the AD design.

2. **Microsoft Consulting has a number of recommendations for creating a good AD design. Which of the following recommendations does Microsoft support?**
   a. Keep the AD design as simple as possible.
   b. The recommended number of forests within an enterprise is one.
   c. The recommended number of domains is one.
   d. All of the above

3. **Users in the Distribution and Manufacturing Departments have been exchanging customer delivery information via e-mail. Customer orders come into the Manufacturing Department from major suppliers. When enough orders have accumulated for a specific drug, the assembly line is configured for that specific medication. The Distribution Department uses the information on the customer's order to ship the product to the appropriate location. How can the Active Directory design resolve this issue?**
   a. Improve user access to resources by putting the users in the same domain.
   b. As long as the Manufacturing Division and the Distribution Division are in the same forest, administrators can assign the appropriate permissions to the required data fields in the order database to allow the users to exchange information.
   c. Do nothing. As long as the Manufacturing Division and the Distribution Division are in the same forest, the users can exchange information.
   d. Allow administrators in the Manufacturing Division and Distribution Division to have administrative permissions in each other's domain.

4. **A manufacturing plant in South Africa only has a dial-up connection. Can they participate in the AD forest?**
   a. No, because you need a high-speed link for AD replication.
   b. No, because you need a high-speed link for authentication.
   c. Yes, authentication and replication can occur over a relatively slow link.
   d. Yes, connectivity should not be an issue in the AD design.

3.2.2 Design an Active Directory naming strategy: Design the namespace

LOGICAL AND PHYSICAL STRUCTURE ELEMENTS

UNDERSTANDING THE OBJECTIVE

AD relies on the DNS to perform name resolution services. Each domain that is created in the AD structure requires a corresponding DNS domain. Because of this requirement, Windows 2000 has a hierarchical structure that can be an exact replica of an existing DNS hierarchy.

WHAT YOU REALLY NEED TO KNOW

◆ The naming strategy should encompass all elements of the network. This includes not just the elements of the AD logical structure but also those from the AD physical structure.

◆ Logical structure elements include forests, trees, domains, organizational units, servers, computers, users, printer objects, or any object that a user could view using the AD Users and Computers tool.

◆ The physical structure elements include sites, site links, site link bridges, subnets, or any element used to document the underlying physical network components.

◆ The forest root domain is the first domain created and begins the naming hierarchy for the first tree in the forest. This is normally the name that is exposed to the outside world if your Windows 2000 and DNS hierarchies follow the same naming pattern. It should therefore be an inclusive name that accurately represents all business units within the organization.

◆ Many networks have only one tree; however, if the circumstances in your enterprise require you to have more than one tree, there will be multiple naming hierarchies in the AD design.

◆ It is possible to have one naming hierarchy that is advertised on the Internet and a separate naming strategy for Windows 2000. This is a decision that must be made before the installation of the first AD domain controller because all other domain controller installations rely on naming schema defined in the first one.

◆ The forest root domain name chosen should be a name that does not change frequently. There should be a high degree of confidence that this is a name that accurately represents the company's products and services to the world for at least the next four years.

OBJECTIVES ON THE JOB

The most important element of a Windows 2000 naming strategy is to create a naming schema that allows users to predict resource names. The most successful naming strategies improve users' productivity by reducing the amount of time users spend searching for resources on the network.

PRACTICE TEST QUESTIONS

1. **Why does the forest root domain name need to be all-inclusive?**
   a. The forest root domain name does not need to be all-inclusive.
   b. All the names used for the Internet domains and Windows 2000 domains must be the same.
   c. If the name is not inclusive, the Windows 2000 domain controllers are not able to replicate.
   d. It represents the company's identity within the organization and can also represent the company's identity externally if the same domain name is used for both Windows 2000 and the DNS that is exposed to the Internet.

2. **When creating the naming strategy, which elements should be included?**
   a. All logical and physical elements
   b. Just the domain controllers and the domains
   c. The forest, trees, and domains
   d. Just the elements that will be exposed on the Internet

3. **Pharmco, Inc. wants to have the same Windows 2000 and Internet identity. What would be the best name for the root of the namespace?**
   a. www.pharmco.com
   b. Enterprise.pharmco.com
   c. Pharmco.com
   d. Pharmco

4. **Pharmco has been expanding the company's presence by acquiring small drug producing companies around the world. Recently, Pharmco acquired a very large producer, Meredith Drugs, which is well-known around the world for the effectiveness of its diabetes and cancer treatments. The company is technologically sophisticated and has a Web interface that allows access to specific information to patients, raw material suppliers, and customers. The technological implementations were an important selling point to Pharmco directors, who want to see the entire company use a similar model. How many name independent namespaces should Pharmco's AD design team plan on having? (Choose all that apply.)**
   a. Just one; Meredith Drugs should be rolled up into the company's Pharmco.com identity.
   b. Two; both the Pharmco and the Meredith Drugs brands represent value and quality.
   c. Just one; create a new company with a completely different name so customers will not be confused.
   d. Create one AD name but have multiple identities on the Internet. This preserves the goodwill value of the Meredith Drugs brand but also simplifies the AD hierarchy.

3.2.3 Design an Active Directory naming strategy: Plan DNS strategy

SERVICE LOCATION RECORDS • REQUESTORS

UNDERSTANDING THE OBJECTIVE

AD relies on specific DNS services to provide seamless access to resources in the AD enterprise. If some of these services are not available, Windows 2000 requires significant additional configuration. Many of the services that can be provided by the Windows 2000 version of DNS enhance the performance and configuration of other network services.

WHAT YOU REALLY NEED TO KNOW

◆ Microsoft uses Service Location Records to passively advertise the location of Windows services to service requestors. The Windows 2000 version of DNS and BIND version 4.9.7 and above support SRV records.

◆ Either a Microsoft Windows 2000 DNS server or a non-Microsoft Windows version of DNS server, such as a BIND server, can provide DNS services. If you are planning to use BIND to provide DNS services for AD, version 8.2.2 is recommended.

◆ DNS services are often managed by a separate group of network administrators responsible for providing WAN services. Network administrators responsible for LAN services generally manage Windows 2000 servers. Because the goals of these two groups of administrators differ (WAN administrators are generally trying to discourage bandwidth usage; whereas, LAN administrators are trying to encourage users to store and access data from LAN servers), it may be difficult to come up with a solution that pleases everyone.

◆ An important decision is whether to use the organization's existing domain name or to create a new Internet identity that can accommodate Windows 2000. It is possible to use the same names but have a separate DNS server to store the AD information for internal use and a second DNS server to be used for external access.

◆ Windows 2000 DNS can be configured to support AD and refer all external requests to a forwarder so that Windows 2000 users have access to all required internal information as well as the Internet.

◆ AD child domains must be created as subdomains in DNS.

OBJECTIVES ON THE JOB

Many organizations have existing DNS servers to support their UNIX or other TCP/IP networking services. This may present a challenge if the version of DNS that is currently in use in your organization does not provide all the services that are provided by a Windows 2000 DNS server. In addition, your company may or may not want to expose the Windows 2000 resources externally.

PRACTICE TEST QUESTIONS

1. **If more than one organization in Pharmco has a well-known Internet identity, does this affect the number of forests that will be created?**
    a. Yes, Pharmco needs a forest for each well-known Internet identity.
    b. It has no effect on the number of forests.
    c. A subdomain is required for each forest.
    d. No, forests and DNS domains have no correlation.

2. **Pharmco has an existing DNS structure in place on several BIND servers. The IT Department has recommended to the AD design team that Windows 2000 DNS be used to support AD so Pharmco can use AD Integrated zones and provide secure dynamic update support for the Windows 2000 clients. The WAN team wants to continue using the existing DNS servers for all other clients. How could this plan be implemented?**
    a. Install Windows 2000 on a non-DC Windows 2000 server.
    b. Install Windows 2000 on a DC, run as a primary server for the AD zones and a secondary for the Internet zones.
    c. It is not possible to implement this scenario.
    d. Update the Windows 2000 domain controllers to native mode. Create the required AD domains on a Windows 2000 domain controller, change the type to AD Integrated, and turn on secure updates. Configure the BIND server as a secondary for the AD zones. Configure the Windows 2000 DNS servers as secondary for the BIND server zones.

3. **Pharmco is planning to provide DNS services for AD using BIND servers. What is the best version of BIND to use?**
    a. BIND version 8.1.2
    b. BIND version 8.2.1
    c. BIND version 8.2.2
    d. BIND version 4.9.7

4. **Pharmco has decided that none of the Windows 2000 AD PCs will be accessed from the Internet. The AD implementation team intends to install Windows 2000 DNS, implement AD Integrated zones, and use the IP addresses of the Windows 2000 domain controllers as the primary DNS servers for the Windows 2000 clients. The Windows 2000 clients also need access to the Internet, but the Windows 2000 server will not be a secondary for the existing BIND servers. How can the Windows 2000 clients access the Internet?**
    a. Install a second NIC and assign the BIND DNS IP address to that NIC.
    b. Set up the Windows 2000 domain controllers, running DNS to forward to the BIND servers.
    c. Configure the IP address of the BIND servers as the alternate DNS server.
    d. This is not a valid implementation.

3.3.1 Design and plan the structure of Organizational Units: Considerations include administration control and administrative policy

ORGANIZATIONAL UNITS • DATA SECURITY

UNDERSTANDING THE OBJECTIVE

Unlike Windows NT, which required a new domain in order to restrict administrative authority to specific sets of resources, Windows 2000 allows domains to be further subdivided into OUs. This allows the number of domains to be reduced and has a significant impact on the replication topology.

WHAT YOU REALLY NEED TO KNOW

◆ Windows 2000 uses OUs as a way of distributing administrative control throughout the organization. Typically, this is control over data security because the users closest to the data generally have the best understanding of how secure data access needs to be.

◆ OUs can also be used to delegate the authority to create AD objects, such as users and computers. If a local LAN administrator has the responsibility for installing PC operating systems or connecting computers to the network, an OU could be created for the specific business unit and the administrator could create all the computer accounts for that OU.

◆ OUs are a good way to add manageability to a large domain. Because a domain can hold between one and two million objects, it makes sense to use another configuration component to organize these objects into manageable groups.

◆ OUs can be used to implement a decentralized IT management strategy. Control can be issued to IT personnel in a matrix management scheme that assigns IT staff to support a fixed set of company resources.

◆ OUs can also be used if the company plans to implement a centralized IT management policy. In this instance, even though IT is centralized, OUs are used to implement IT management objectives, such as the application of group policy or the creation of containers that hold resources that will be accessed remotely.

OBJECTIVES ON THE JOB

Organizations have many different ways of implementing administration. In the past, Windows NT domains have forced the creation of many different domains in the network, solely to create administrative units, due to the limitations of security administration in the NT environment. Windows 2000 allows organizations to compress the number of independent domains but continues to maintain the autonomy of data security.

PRACTICE TEST QUESTIONS

1. Pharmco is analyzing the company's structure to determine what form of IT administration would best service the company's needs. The AD design team is planning to create a number of different administrative scenarios and apply them in the test environment to see how well each performs. In the first scenario, all IT functions are centralized, and software is installed on all PCs in the company to enable them to be controlled remotely. Windows 2000 has been standardized on all PCs, and users must submit requests for new software to the IT Department for approval before it can be installed on a PC in the Pharmco network. All IT staff will be cross-trained so they can correct most problems that arise. Given this information, how could AD be designed to implement this scenario?
   a. Create a different domain for each geographic location.
   b. Assign locations to each IT staff member, and create a different domain for each location.
   c. Create an OU for each IT staff member, and put all the objects they will manage in the OU.
   d. Create one domain, and create OUs to make it easier to manage the large number of objects. All IT staff will be members of the Domain Admins group in the forest root domain.

2. In the second scenario, IT is planning to centralize all the domain configuration and physical structure configuration, but delegate responsibility for user and computer object creation to the business units. Which AD design best supports this administrative policy?
   a. Single domain, no OUs
   b. Single domain, one OU for each location
   c. Single domain, one OU for each business unit
   d. Single forest, one domain for each business unit

3. In the third scenario, IT wants to maintain centralized control of domain configuration, physical structure configuration, and object creation. However, IT wants to delegate some of the ongoing network administration, such as password resets and printer document management, to the business units. What is the best AD design to support these criteria?
   a. Single forest, one domain for each business unit
   b. Single forest, one domain, one OU for each business unit
   c. Single forest, single domain, one OU for IT, one OU for each business unit
   d. Single forest, one tree for IT, one tree for each business unit

4. What is the most important function of OUs in an AD structure?
   a. To eliminate single points of failure
   b. To decrease network bandwidth due to authentication
   c. To improve work group interaction
   d. To allow administrative policy to be applied to the organization, to enable delegation of administrative authority, and to organize objects into manageable units

OBJECTIVES

3.3.2 Design and plan the structure of Organizational Units: Considerations include existing resource domains and geographic and company structure

EXISTING DOMAINS • DOCUMENTATION • GEOGRAPHICAL BOUNDARIES

UNDERSTANDING THE OBJECTIVE

OUs are typically used to implement Windows 2000 administrative policies. In many instances, however, organizations have an existing NT domain environment, a specific geographical presence, and an existing management structure that further defines where OUs are required.

WHAT YOU REALLY NEED TO KNOW

- ◆ Examine the network documentation that was gathered during the data collection phase of the design. Analyze the organization's existing network structure, and identify any servers that need to be migrated to Windows 2000. Identify all NT domains and determine which of these can be rolled up into OUs.

- ◆ The changes that occur in the world's economic environment affect all companies, and this trickles down to the network. As a result, many networks (especially over the last five years) have taken on a multi-national flavor. This can have a profound effect on AD.

- ◆ The new geographical element, that used to be reserved for only the largest of companies, adds another element to the design of AD. Specifically, administrators must determine how to implement network policies that support the varied cultural and language differences at company locations. In a small to medium-sized company, OUs can be used to represent these geographic boundaries.

- ◆ OUs based on geographic boundaries can assist network administrators in planning and applying group policies that implement OS installations, which provide for different desktop and software configurations that take into account language, currency representations, and other cultural differences.

- ◆ Some companies are organized based largely on function, and, although resources may be geographically dispersed, the users in the functional units require access to the same software, data, and other resources.

OBJECTIVES ON THE JOB

One of the easiest ways to determine where OUs should be created is to look at your existing NT environment. Many company implementations include one or more account domains and numerous other NT resources domains. If your organization plans to retain the same network administration policies, the account domains can be rolled up into one forest root domain, and the NT resource domains can become OUs. Although there are other ways to implement this type of structure, most of them are variations on this same scheme.

PRACTICE TEST QUESTIONS

1. **The network environment at Pharmco has become very unwieldy over the past several years, as the company has expanded its overseas operations dramatically. As a result, there are now NT domains at every major geographic location, and this has created barriers to data sharing because onsite network administrators are not always able to convince their counterparts in other locations to create the trust relationships necessary to allow resource access. As a result, many users have multiple user IDs to access information in remote NT domains. What feature of AD overcomes this problem?**
    a. Automatic transitive trusts
    b. Transitive trusts created by the forest root Enterprise Administrators group
    c. Shortcut trusts
    d. Explicit trusts

2. **Pharmco wants to reduce the overall number of domains that are deployed around the world. The AD design team wants to ensure that domains are only created when absolutely necessary. Accordingly, the following guidelines have been issued. Create domains only when: (1) a separate security policy is required or (2) bandwidth is limited to such an extent that replication traffic needs to be kept to an absolute minimum. Both the Accounting and HR Departments have specified complex passwords with short password expiration periods. Using these guidelines, what is the minimum number of domains and OUs Pharmco should create?**
    a. One domain and one OU for each department that needs a separate security policy
    b. Two domains and one OU for each geographical region
    c. Two domains and one OU for each set of objects that will be administered as a group
    d. One domain and two OUs

3. **Pharmco has organized the Operations Division so that each geographical region has a local component. The company is currently divided into the following regions: Asia, North American Operations, and Europe. The Operations Division is divided into Accounting, Human Resources, and Corporate Management. Should OUs be created based upon location or functional activities?**
    a. OUs should be based upon geography, due to bandwidth limitations for replication.
    b. OUs should be based upon geography because they all share the same languages.
    c. OUs should be based upon functional activities because it is easier to manage.
    d. OUs should be based upon functional activities because users performing the same functions need access to the same resources.

3.3.3 Design and plan the structure of Organizational Units: Develop an OU delegation plan

DELEGATION OF AUTHORITY WIZARD

UNDERSTANDING THE OBJECTIVE

Centralized IT functions play a very important role in maintaining the stability of the company's network infrastructure. However, corporate IT departments face many challenges in trying to maintain a well-trained workforce, deliver timely services, and keep pace with company growth. Delegation of authority is one way corporate IT departments can leverage resources within strategic business units to provide support for repetitive tasks that do not affect the overall level of service to the network as a whole.

WHAT YOU REALLY NEED TO KNOW

- ◆ Users can be delegated the authority to manage a portion of the network environment or just the authority to manage specific objects or object properties.

- ◆ Companies should use delegation of authority as a way to reduce the number of calls that must be resolved by a central help desk. Calls should continue to be tracked by the help desk for planning purposes, but requests for assistance can be routed to a local administrator within an OU that has been assigned specific privileges to perform tasks, such as password or other property changes.

- ◆ If the IT Department has a hybrid design in which some functions are performed centrally and others are performed in local strategic business units, the delegation of authority feature allows the local administrators to easily be assigned permissions to manage a set of objects, even if their own user object exists in another container.

- ◆ The Delegation of Authority Wizard allows domain administrators to select and delegate pre-defined or custom tasks. This prevents task administrators from receiving permissions to objects or properties that are not under their administrative purview.

- ◆ Users who create objects in AD are, by default, members of the Creator Owners group and have full control over any objects they create.

- ◆ Network administration that is based on function may affect the design of AD. If the IT Department wants to assign technicians to service and maintain users' PCs, it may be easiest to create all the PCs in OUs.

- ◆ Delegation of authority can also be assigned for the creation and application of group policy objects.

OBJECTIVES ON THE JOB

Delegation of authority can perform a number of functions within a network environment. First, it can off-load repetitive tasks from a highly skilled group of technical workers, so that those workers can focus on tasks that affect the entire network. Second, it creates a pool of workers, from which to draw new technical talent, who have acquired on-the-job experience with some part of the organization's network.

PRACTICE TEST QUESTIONS

1. **Does the user object for the person being delegated authority need to exist in the same container as the objects he or she will be managing?**
   - a. Yes, you cannot manage objects in a remote OU.
   - b. No, a user's object does not need to be in the same container they are administering.
   - c. Yes, this limits the scope of the delegation.
   - d. Yes, this allows the user to see the objects to be managed.

2. **Pharmco's AD design team wants to create an OU delegation policy that allows local container administrators to create and manage objects in their assigned containers and leaves all global AD configurations to administrators in the central IT organization. You have been assigned to perform the delegation of authority to implement this plan. Do you need to create a pre-defined or custom delegation?**
   - a. Custom, because this is for all objects in the container
   - b. Custom, because you cannot assign this type of delegation of authority with a pre-defined delegation
   - c. Pre-defined, because this is a delegation that was envisioned by Microsoft
   - d. Pre-defined, because it does not require a change to the schema

3. **Can a user be delegated the authority to change the properties of an OU?**
   - a. Yes, a user can be assigned permission to manipulate the GPOs that are assigned to an OU.
   - b. Yes, users can be assigned change permissions to an OU.
   - c. No, you cannot use the Delegation of Authority Wizard to do this.
   - d. No, you can only be assigned permissions, not delegated authority.

4. **Can a user be delegated the authority to manage just user objects, or must they be delegated the authority to manage all resources in a container at the same time?**
   - a. Users must be assigned authority for either all objects or all attributes.
   - b. Users cannot be assigned authority for all objects, but they can be delegated authority for all the attributes of one object class.
   - c. You cannot manage just user objects because each user must have a PC.
   - d. Users can be delegated authority to manage just one or two specific classes of objects using the Delegation of Authority Wizard.

5. **Can a user be delegated the authority to reset other users' passwords?**
   - a. You cannot delegate password changes because this is a security option.
   - b. You can only change user passwords if you are a domain administrator.
   - c. This is a common administrative task that could easily be performed by a container administrator.
   - d. No, users would not want the container administrator to know their passwords.

3.3.4 Design and plan the structure of Organizational Units: Plan group policy object management

GROUP POLICY

UNDERSTANDING THE OBJECTIVE

Group policies are similar to system policies under Windows NT. However, the role of group policies under Windows 2000 is more far-reaching. Rather that using policies simply to control users' desktops, group policies are the focal point for control over how to deliver software, desktop settings, and data access to users, regardless of their current location in the network.

WHAT YOU REALLY NEED TO KNOW

◆ A group policy can be assigned to any container in the AD. Assigning a GPO to a container is referred to as linking. When a GPO is created, it is automatically assigned or linked to the container in which it is created.

◆ AD contains a default group called the Group Policy Admins group. The members of this group are automatically defined as the Creator Owner of the GPO and therefore have full control over the GPO. If a user who is a member of the Domain Admins group creates a GPO, the Domain Admins group becomes the Creator Owner.

◆ By default, the Authenticated Users group has *Read* and *Apply Group Policy* permissions. This means a GPO can affect all users and computers in the container. If the administrator's user account or computer is a member of the container to which the GPO is applied, the Apply Group Policy setting should be turned off for that object.

◆ Group policies can affect the length of time it takes a user to log on. Due to inheritance, it is possible to have multiple GPOs assigned to the same user or PC. The object could have a policy applied at the site, domain, parent OU, or object OU level. At each container, a check is made to see if there are either computer or user policies to be applied. Depending on the number of levels in the hierarchy, the user could experience a delay in the logon process.

◆ In the event of a conflict, GPOs applied closer to the user take precedence by default. However, group policy options can be assigned that limit this default action and cause a GPO that is processed at a higher level in the hierarchy to take precedence. This option is known as No Override.

OBJECTIVES ON THE JOB

Designing and implementing group policies in an enterprise environment can be a challenging task, requiring knowledge about the network infrastructure and how to use the Group Policy Editor, as well as an in-depth knowledge of security protocols, software installation, and the desktop environment. The organization needs to determine not only which group policy objects to create, but also how to distribute and manage the objects in a way that does not have a negative impact on other network operations.

PRACTICE TEST QUESTIONS

1. **The IT Department wants to delegate the ability to create group policy objects to users in each OU. However, IT does not want these users to be able to edit or delete GPOs created by users in other containers. What is the best way to implement this task?**
   a. Assign the users with the responsibility to create the GPOs members of the Domain Admins group.
   b. Assign the users with the responsibility to create the GPOs members of the Group Policy Admins group.
   c. Assign the users with the responsibility to create the GPOs members of the Enterprise Admins group.
   d. Use the Delegate Control Wizard to give the users with the responsibility to create GPOs full control to all the user objects in the container.

2. **The following object exists in the Pharmco AD forest: CN=Kadams, CN=parts, CN=manuf, DC=Asia, DC=Pharmco, DC=com. Group policy objects have been applied at the site, subdomain, and child OU level. How many GPOs will be applied to this object?**
   a. One
   b. Two
   c. Three
   d. Six

3. **The following object exists in the Pharmco AD forest: CN=Kadams, CN=parts, CN=manuf, DC=Asia, DC=Pharmco, DC=com. If GPOs have been applied at all levels of the AD hierarchy, how many GPOs will be applied to this object?**
   a. Two OUs, two domains, one site
   b. Two OUs, three domains, one site
   c. Three OUs, two domains, one site
   d. Three OUs, three domains, one site

4. **Pharmco has created a group policy hierarchy. A site-level policy assigns a time card application, and a domain-level policy removes the Run Command from the Start Menu. An OU-level policy disables the policy item that removes the Run Command from the Start Menu. Does the Run Command appear on the Start Menu?**
   a. Yes, because the GPO in the container closest to the object takes precedence.
   b. No, because the GPO items in the site level policy takes precedence.
   c. No, because the GPO items in the domain level policy take precedence.
   d. There is not enough information to decide.

3.3.5 Design and plan the structure of Organizational Units: Plan policy management for client computers

POLICY MANAGEMENT

UNDERSTANDING THE OBJECTIVE

Group policy can be managed either in a global or decentralized fashion. Certain types of policies lend themselves to one of these two categories. Establishing the appropriate management design for the creation of policies and updates is needed to keep the policy focused on supporting business objectives and is an important element of the overall AD design.

WHAT YOU REALLY NEED TO KNOW

◆ When designing a group policy, the first criterion that must be determined is the policy scope. Scope determines whether the policy is applied domain-wide or whether it pertains to just one or more OU.

◆ Certain security policy items, such as account policies and public key policies, have domain-wide scope. In other words, these policies cannot be applied to just one OU.

◆ Account policies include the password policy, account lockout policy, and the Kerberos policy. The Kerberos policy can only be accessed from the property sheet of the domain object.

◆ Except for public key policies, all policies are assigned to the computer configuration rather than to the user configuration. Public key policies can be assigned to both the user and computer configuration.

◆ Although password policy and account lockout policy items are available at the OU level, when linked to an OU, they only pertain to users who log on locally to the PCs that are affected by the resulting group policy.

◆ One way to assign group policy is to create OUs that organize PCs based upon function. For example, all e-mail servers or application servers could be in one OU. Another OU could contain all the RIS servers. An example of this is the domain controller's OU created in each domain. By default, all domain controllers in a domain have an object in this container.

OBJECTIVES ON THE JOB

Certain types of policies lend themselves to either a global or local design strategy. For example, security policies are generally something that is left to the centralized IT team because it is something that affects the overall company business. Policies that determine which icons should be on a particular group of users' desktops are something that requires local knowledge. The IT Department may also want to push policies that the security system files on users' desktops or restrict access to the Registry. These kinds of policies further protect company assets, even if a user inadvertently leaves the desktop exposed.

PRACTICE TEST QUESTIONS

1. **Pharmco has created an AD design that includes three levels of OUs—geographical regions, strategic business units, and functional departments. The Distribution Division in the Asia-Pacific region wants to assign a security policy that restricts the membership of the administrators group on the local PCs. The OU administrators in the accounting OU want to have different members. Which GPO will be implemented, the strategic business unit OU GPO or the departmental OU?**
   a. Neither, security policies can only be created at the domain level.
   b. Neither, security policies have domain-wide scope and do not apply to the PCs in the OUs.
   c. Departmental OU due to inheritance
   d. Strategic business unit OU

2. **What will happen if a No Override is set at the departmental OU?**
   a. Nothing, the security policy can only be set at the domain.
   b. The departmental OU GPO will be implemented.
   c. The strategic business unit OU GPO will be implemented.
   d. The departmental OU cannot set a No Override option.

3. **Will there be any change in the application of the GPOs if a No Override is set at the strategic business unit level?**
   a. No, the domain security policy is the only one that can be set.
   b. No, the departmental OU GPO will be implemented due to inheritance.
   c. Both GPOs will be applied to the affected PCs.
   d. The strategic business unit OU GPO will be applied.

4. **The GPO designed in Question 1 has been set to be disabled at the strategic business unit level. However, it is linked to the domain container. What effect will this have on the application of the two conflicting policies?**
   a. It will not be applied at the strategic business unit level.
   b. The domain policy will take precedence because security level policies can only be implemented from the domain.
   c. The departmental OU GPO will be implemented due to inheritance.
   d. The GPO will not be applied because when it is disabled at one level; it cannot be implemented at another level until the disable option is removed.

5. **The IT Department wants to control access to the system files on all the application servers in the Asia-Pacific region. How can this be accomplished? (Choose all that apply.)**
   a. Create the GPO at the departmental OU level, and link it to the domain.
   b. Create the GPO at the domain level.
   c. Create a new OU, and move all application servers into the new OU. Create the GPO in the new OU.
   d. Create a new OU, and move all application servers into the new OU. Create the GPO in the domain container. Disable the GPO in the domain container, and link it to the new OU.

3.4.1 Plan for the coexistence of Active Directory and other directory services: Plan a WINS strategy

WINS • DATAGRAMS • NETBIOS

UNDERSTANDING THE OBJECTIVE

Although the WINS takes a back seat to the DNS in the AD enterprise, WINS services are still required to ensure that you have the appropriate name resolution support for the existing NetBIOS environment. Many client PC and network applications still rely on NetBIOS as the primary name resolution mechanism.

WHAT YOU REALLY NEED TO KNOW

♦ WINS allows clients to send directed datagrams to perform lookup services for the NetBIOS name to IP address resolution. The resulting destination IP address is used to perform an ARP lookup to resolve the IP address for a physical layer (MAC) address.

♦ WINS can be supported on the same servers that provide DNS services. Both services can be configured to forward unresolved requests to the other service for possible name resolution. For example, a WINS server could forward a WINS request to a DNS server to see if the DNS server has a record that could resolve the name resolution request.

♦ Windows 2000 servers must register with WINS servers, or any of the down-level (Windows) clients will not be able to locate them as resources in the network. This can be done one of two ways. The first way is to modify the properties of the TCP/IP protocol to configure the servers as WINS clients. This creates a record in the WINS database. The second way is to configure the WINS server to forward any unresolved requests to the DNS server.

♦ Windows 2000 professional clients will also not register with a WINS server by default unless configured as DHCP clients. The DHCP server must be configured with the IP address of a WINS server. Otherwise, users are not able to easily share resources from their local PCs.

OBJECTIVES ON THE JOB

Windows for Workgroups, Windows 95/98, and Windows NT rely on WINS to provide name resolution services. These operating systems are all browser-based, meaning they rely on an election process to assign browser roles for each subnet. Each browser is responsible for a certain task in the resource location process. For example, a backup browser provides a list of available resources to the clients. This system is used when a client does not know where a resource resides; after a resource location is identified, the client needs to make a request to the server service of a specific host.

PRACTICE TEST QUESTIONS

1. **Pharmco has designed an AD infrastructure that encompasses the entire enterprise. Now that the logical design phase is completed, the architects need to consider the AD physical infrastructure and the network services required to support all hosts on the network. There will be a mix of Windows 2000 and Windows 95/98/NT clients. Will WINS servers be needed on the network?**
   a. No, because all of these clients can use DNS to resolve computer names.
   b. No, because name resolution is not necessary.
   c. Yes, but only for the Windows 95 PCs.
   d. Yes, for name resolution for the Windows 95/98/NT PCs.

2. **Pharmco has installed a new SQL Server 2000 database server on the factory floor of a manufacturing plant in Tunis. The technician installed and tested the new database application that controls the production line for a new diabetes medication. He tested connectivity to the database using his new laptop computer and had no problems connecting to the server. However, three production line managers, who need to monitor the activity of the production line from their offices, are not able to connect even though they were able to connect to the older SQL server. The technician is using Windows 2000 Professional on the laptop. Both the laptop and the SQL server are registered in DNS. The managers' PCs are using WINS for name resolution. Why can the technician connect to the server, but the managers cannot?**
   a. The SQL server needs to be configured as a WINS client.
   b. The SQL server needs to be configured as a WINS server.
   c. The SQL server needs to be configured as a DNS server.
   d. The SQL server needs to be configured as a DNS client.

3. **One of the managers at the manufacturing plant in Tunis has had her PC upgraded to Windows 2000 Professional. The manager has a production levels application on her PC that is accessed by the shift supervisors to keep her updated about production levels on each shift. The shift supervisors were unable to access the application last night. In fact, her PC could not be seen when browsing. What is the problem? (Choose all that apply.)**
   a. The Windows 2000 Professional PC has the wrong IP address.
   b. The Windows 2000 Professional PC is not a WINS client and is behind a router that is preventing NetBIOS broadcasts.
   c. The Windows 2000 Professional PC is not in the DNS database.
   d. The Windows 2000 Professional PC is not a DHCP client.

3.4.2 Plan for the coexistence of Active Directory and other directory services: Plan a DHCP strategy

DHCP • USER CLASS • VENDOR CLASS • NETSH

UNDERSTANDING THE OBJECTIVE

DHCP provides a number of new services in the Windows 2000 environment, and many of them relate to support of DNS. DHCP supports a new feature of DNS called Dynamic DNS. This means that administrators no longer have to manually enter host records in the DNS database, leading to fewer errors and more reliable name resolution services.

WHAT YOU REALLY NEED TO KNOW

- ◆ DHCP can fill a DNS database with records from DHCP clients. By default, all Windows 2000 clients register a record with a Windows 2000 DNS server or any DNS server configured to accept dynamic updates.

- ◆ DHCP can be configured to apply different DNS options to members of a predefined User or Vendor Class. This allows PCs sharing the same scope to be assigned different options, such as routers and name servers, for load balancing purposes.

- ◆ Under Windows NT, the rule for creating a scope was to put 75 percent of the IP addresses for a specific range in one DHCP server and the other 25 percent of the IP addresses for that same range in another DHCP server. This was to create a backup server to be used in case the DHCP server for a specific subnet went down. In Windows 2000, per the Windows 2000 Server Resource Kit, this has been changed to the 80/20 rule.

- ◆ In Windows 2000, all DHCP servers pass DHCPInform packets every five minutes to announce themselves as authorized DHCP servers. In an AD domain, every DHCP server that is installed and configured on the network must be authorized to provide DHCP services. A member of the Enterprise Administrators group completes this task. This prevents users from bringing up rogue DHCP servers. DHCP servers that are running Windows NT do not check for authorization.

- ◆ If you need to script the configuration of a DHCP server, use the Netsh command. Netsh is a multi-level command environment that allows services to be managed in a non-console environment. Use the Netsh DHCP mode to dump the configuration of an existing DHCP server. Save this as a backup for rebuilding a copy of this server.

OBJECTIVES ON THE JOB

DHCP is generally the service that identifies the IP address of a server providing DNS services. A Windows 2000 DHCP server can offer DDNS services to downlevel clients that do not have these capabilities included in their current TCP/IP stack.

PRACTICE TEST QUESTIONS

1. **Pharmco decided to implement a phased installation plan for the upgrade to Windows 2000. Eventually, all clients and servers will be running Windows 2000. In the first phase, all the domain controllers were upgraded to Windows 2000. In the second phase, all the PCs were upgraded to Windows 2000 Professional. The Help Desk is starting to receive a high volume of calls from the two sites that were upgraded over the weekend. One of the problems is that the Windows 2000 Professional clients are not able to PING existing Windows NT servers. The servers are configured to be DHCP and WINS clients. What is the best way to correct this problem?**
   - a. Make the NT servers WINS servers rather than clients.
   - b. Make the NT servers DHCP servers rather than clients.
   - c. Configure the Windows 2000 DHCP servers to enable updates for clients that do not support dynamic updates.
   - d. Create static host entries in the DNS database.

2. **Pharmco needs to configure a TCP/IP network at a site that will not have connectivity to the corporate WAN initially. They plan to put local WINS and DHCP servers and an AD domain controller from the Pharmco domain at the local site. What is the fastest and easiest way to deploy the DHCP server at the local site?**
   - a. Install DHCP, and configure the scope and all the options as necessary.
   - b. Use Netsh to do a DHCP dump on an existing DHCP server, and create a script using the results of the dump to configure the new DHCP server.
   - c. Use the DHCP manager to create an automated installation script.
   - d. Use Sysprep to create an automated installation script and include a UDF for the configuration of the DHCP server.

3. **Pharmco created a new DHCP implementation scheme that employs loadbalancing techniques for all scopes, supports DDNS, and optimizes resource usage on the network by combining the DHCP and WINS services on the same servers. One of the technicians in the IT Department was doing a daily check on the client lease databases of the new servers and discovered that one of the servers did not have any client leases issued. The scope was activated, and all routers in the network are configured to allow the DHCP packets to pass. How can this problem be corrected?**
   - a. Authorize the DHCP server in the AD domain.
   - b. Install a DHCP relay agent.
   - c. Change the scope options to add a router address.
   - d. Use the 80/20 rule to configure the DHCP server.

4. **Where is a DHCP relay agent configured in Windows 2000?**
   - a. In the DHCP manager
   - b. In the DNS manager
   - c. In Network and Dial-up connections
   - d. In the RRAS server

3.5.1 Design an Active Directory site topology: Design a replication strategy

REPLICATION • INTRA-SITE • INTER-SITE

UNDERSTANDING THE OBJECTIVE

AD moves away from the single master model of the NT domains to a multi-master model that leaves all domain controllers available for new object creation, property updates, and configuration and schema changes. In essence, rather than having just one writable copy of the domain database, every domain controller is writable.

WHAT YOU REALLY NEED TO KNOW

- ◆ Replication is the process of sending information from one domain controller to one or more additional domain controllers. Replication is controlled automatically within AD by a service called the KCC.

- ◆ Replication is currently divided into two separate replication schemes. One scheme is for intra-site in which domain controllers notify each other within five minutes of making a change.

- ◆ The second scheme is for inter-site replication. Inter-site is replication between domain controllers that are separated by a site boundary either because of low bandwidth or the amount of replication control needed to achieve convergence.

- ◆ AD replication occurs at the attribute level. If a change is made to the property of an object, only the property is replicated to other domain controllers not the entire object.

- ◆ AD divides data into manageable sets called partitions. There are three writable partitions: Schema, Configuration, and Domain. The kind of data that is changed determines the partition it affects and which domain controllers need to receive the changes. These partitions are also referred to as Naming Contexts.

- ◆ Changes made to objects in the domain partition are only replicated to other domain controllers in the same domain. Creating new domain objects, such as users or shared folders, or changing any of the attributes on the property pages of an object causes domain partition replication.

- ◆ Changes made to objects in the schema or configuration partition must be replicated to every domain controller in the entire enterprise.

OBJECTIVES ON THE JOB

In an enterprise environment, having only a single point from which to generate updates would be unworkable. In a directory service, the amount of data that can be associated with a single object grows exponentially, so you need a design that accommodates multiple points of access. This leads to the next issue, sending the resulting updates to the rest of the participating members of the domain, the domain controllers via replication.

PRACTICE TEST QUESTIONS

1. **The AD design team at Pharmco is concerned that replication traffic between domains will reduce bandwidth availability to existing applications. Pharmco, Inc. proposed design shows a three site physical AD network, including a EuroAmerica site, an Asia-Pacific site, and a South American site. To ensure that replication traffic does not affect bandwidth availability for applications, which of the following replication strategies should be employed?**
   a. Create one domain each for Europe, North America, South America, and Asia-Pacific regions.
   b. Create one domain for South America, one for Asia-Pacific, and one for Europe and North America combined.
   c. Create one domain for Europe-North America and one for Asia-South America.
   d. The domain structure does not matter because the schema and configuration partitions update domain controllers in all sites in the entire forest.

2. **Pharmco has a proposed design that includes a total of 22 domain controllers in the entire forest. The DCs are divided into three domains created along site boundaries. If an administrator changes the password for a user object in the SA domain, how many domain controllers will receive this change via replication?**
   a. Six – Four domain controllers in SA and one bridgehead server in NA and Asia must receive this change.
   b. 22 – All domain controllers must receive this change.
   c. Seven – Four domain controllers in SA and one bridgehead server in each of the three sites must receive this change.
   d. Four – All domain controllers in SA where the user object exists must receive this change.

3. **AD has separate replication topologies for certain kinds of AD information. In an AD design with three domains and three sites, how many replication topologies exist?**
   a. Four – One for each domain and one for the schema and configuration partitions
   b. Five – One for each domain, one for the configuration partition, and one for the schema partition
   c. Three – One for the domains and one each for the configuration and schema partitions
   d. Two – One for the domains and one for the schema and configuration partitions

4. **A new domain has been created for Meredith Drugs. How many DCs need to receive this change? (Choose all that apply.)**
   a. All the DCs in the forest
   b. Only the DCs in the Meredith Drugs domain
   c. All DCs in the new domain and one bridgehead server in each site
   d. Only the DCs that hold the configuration partition

3.5.2 Design an Active Directory site topology: Define site boundaries

SITE BOUNDARIES

UNDERSTANDING THE OBJECTIVE

AD has two distinct structures. The first is a logical structure comprised of a forest of trees, domains, and OUs. The second is a physical structure comprised of sites and domain controllers. Sites represent the physical architecture of our network topology and, when defined properly, can significantly improve bandwidth utilization statistics related to AD.

WHAT YOU REALLY NEED TO KNOW

- ◆ Site boundaries limit the flow of replication data between segments of the enterprise to the schedule and intervals assigned by an administrator.

- ◆ Replication does not occur between sites automatically as intra-site replication does. Rather, the network administrator must create an object known as a site link before the Inter-site Topology Generator will be able to create the connection points needed to foster replication between sites. The ISTG is the first DC created in a site.

- ◆ Sites can also be used to control logon traffic, FRS updates, and the Distributed File system topology. Replication within sites is uncompressed. Inter-site replication is compressed to within 15 percent of its original size.

- ◆ The KCC runs every 15 minutes on each domain controller to check for topology changes. If no changes occur within a six-hour period on a domain controller, the replication process is kicked off as an insurance mechanism.

- ◆ There are multiple replication topologies. The schema and configuration naming contexts (partitions) share a replication topology because they are both enterprise wide. Each domain has its own replication topology. A forest of three domains would have four replication topologies.

- ◆ The point of involving an administrator to manually create site links is to provide control over the traffic passing across relatively expensive WAN links. Each site link has an associated cost parameter that defines how expensive it is to send data across that link versus another.

- ◆ Use site link bridges to define a path between two distant sites using site links.

OBJECTIVES ON THE JOB

A site is a group of well-connected subnets that define the boundaries for AD replication. The goal of a good AD design should be to create an enterprise environment that meets the business needs of the organization and the administrative needs of the IT Department as well as create a physical design that results in an efficient replication topology. Replication has a significant impact on network operations both from a bandwidth standpoint and a data consistency standpoint.

PRACTICE TEST QUESTIONS

1. **The IT Department in Corporate Operations has had only limited training regarding AD replication. However, some team members remember reading an article from an IT publication that said the Knowledge Consistency Checker would automatically create the connection objects for replication. The Human Resources Department in Corporate Operations recently updated the AD schema to add a new attribute, employee number, to the user object. When administrators in the OUs not located in the EuroAmerica site try to use this attribute, it is not available. What needs to be done for administrators in the remote AD sites to use this attribute?**
   a. Update all the links between sites to T-3 so replication traffic is received more quickly.
   b. Create manual connection objects between the three sites.
   c. Create a site link bridge between all three sites.
   d. Create site links between the EuroAmerica site and the SA and Asia-Pacific sites.

2. **Members of the IT Department at Pharmco are concerned that AD replication traffic will use too much bandwidth on an expensive T-3 link that has been installed between the South American and European LANs to support a new replicated database application. How can the IT Department ensure that AD uses the link efficiently?**
   a. Create separate AD sites for domain controllers in North America and Europe. Create a link between NA, Europe, and SA, and a second site link between SA and Europe. Set the cost to use the site link between SA and Europe to be higher that the link between NA, Europe, and SA.
   b. Create a manual connection between Europe and SA.
   c. Create a site between SA and Europe so all traffic is local.
   d. Do not do anything different. AD will automatically choose the correct link.

3. **Members of Pharmco's IT Department are concerned that workstation logon traffic is competing with application traffic across the existing T3 link. How can site topology reduce the workstation logon traffic across this link?**
   a. Add an additional T-3 link to provide more bandwidth.
   b. Create a site for North America and one for Europe. Make sure that domain controllers exist in the site for the domains to which the workstations are authenticating. Make sure all clients are site-aware.
   c. Create a separate site in Europe just for all the workstations.
   d. Upgrade all the workstations to Windows 2000 Professional.

4. **How can downlevel workstations be made site-aware? (Choose all that apply.)**
   a. Upgrade them to Windows 2000 Professional.
   b. Install the AD Workstation Upgrade Pack.
   c. Install the AD Client Extensions.
   d. Change the properties of the workstation object in Active Directory Users and Computers.

3.6 Design a Schema Modification Policy

ACTIVE DIRECTORY SCHEMA • CLASSES • ATTRIBUTES

UNDERSTANDING THE OBJECTIVE

The AD schema is similar to a data dictionary in that it defines all the current object classes and attributes that exist or can be exploited by the AD database. The schema should be relatively stable, requiring few changes or updates. However, when updates do occur, the entire AD forest is impacted because changes to the schema must be replicated to all domain controllers within a forest.

WHAT YOU REALLY NEED TO KNOW

♦ By default, schema modification is a centralized function that exists with the Schema Administrators group in the forest root domain. Membership in this group should be restricted. By default, the only user account with authority to change the schema is the administrator account in the first domain to be installed in the forest.

♦ The schema can be modified using the AD Schema tool or by scripting tools such as ADSIEdit. The committee should approve all changes.

♦ Objects and attributes added to the schema can be deactivated but never deleted. This makes a strong case for careful analysis prior to allowing any schema changes.

♦ Two types of components can be added to AD: classes and attributes. A class is a component that shares a common set of attributes, for example, users or printers. Attributes define the properties of a particular class object. An example of a user attribute is a telephone number or address.

♦ Changes to the schema should first be implemented in a test environment to ensure that errors are not introduced into the production directory service.

♦ Schema modification should be scheduled with all domain administrators in the forest because it is possible for an instance of a new class to be created on one domain controller before the new class definition has been replicated to all domain controllers within AD. An appropriate recovery plan must be developed.

♦ Installation programs for directory-enabled applications that need to modify the schema should be written in two parts: one for the schema update and another for the software setup. Schema administrators perform the first part, and technicians perform the second.

OBJECTIVES ON THE JOB

There are two primary reasons to change the AD schema. The first is when the organization has a unique object type or attribute function that cannot be adequately addressed by existing AD objects or their associated properties. The second situation occurs when an AD-enabled application is installed and requires custom objects to be used by the new service. E-mail server software is an example of an application that may need to change the schema to define SMTP or X.400 objects used in mail delivery.

PRACTICE TEST QUESTIONS

1. **A technician in the Accounting Department has been given the task of installing a new payroll application that is designed to work with Windows 2000 and AD. When the installation package runs, it asks the technician to log on with an account that has permissions to modify the schema. To what group does the user need to be a member, and how should this application installation be handled?**
   a. The user needs to be a member of the Domain Administrators group in the accounting domain and install the application during off hours.
   b. The user needs to be a member of the Domain Administrators group in the accounting domain and install the application during regular business hours.
   c. The user needs to be a member of Schema administrators group. A member of the Schema administrators group should run the application during off hours until it completes the AD schema changes. The technician can then install the rest of the application.
   d. The user needs to be a member of the Domain Administrators group in the forest root domain. A member of the Domain Administrators group should run the application during regular business hours until it completes the AD schema changes. The technician can then install the rest of the application.

2. **The administrator account for the forest root domain is used to start the installation of the new payroll application. However, the installation fails with an error about write permissions. What needs to be done to ensure the administrator has the rights needed to install the Payroll application?**
   a. Use the AD Schema tool to open the Operations Master properties page, and select Change Schema permissions on the domain.
   b. Use the AD Schema tool to open the Operations Master properties page, and select The Schema may be modified on this domain controller.
   c. Have a member of the Schema Admins group run the installation.
   d. Have a member of the Domain Admins group, where the application is being installed, run the installation.

3. **The AD Change Committee approved a request to change the AD to add an attribute called employee number to the user class. A technician on the night shift ran the script to make the change. After running the script, the technician tried to add test user to be sure the new attribute was accessible. On the new custom property page, the attribute appears as ENPLOYEE NUMBER. How can the spelling of the attribute be corrected, and what can be done to prevent errors in the future?**
   a. Change the spelling in the script, rerun it in a test environment, and then rerun in the production environment. This corrects the attribute in AD.
   b. Delete the incorrect attribute in the script, create a new attribute in the script, and then rerun it in a test environment.
   c. Change the spelling in the script, and rerun it in the production environment.
   d. The attribute cannot be removed, only deactivated. Test scripts in test environment before running in the production environment.

3.7.1 Design an Active Directory implementation plan: Design a single domain structure

SINGLE DOMAIN STRUCTURE

UNDERSTANDING THE OBJECTIVE

Understanding the basic features of AD provides a designer with the information needed to create an initial AD design. Most AD designs are relatively simple, reflecting the multitude of small to medium size businesses that drive our capitalist economy.

WHAT YOU REALLY NEED TO KNOW

- ◆ Because domains are used to establish security boundaries, objects within the domain share a single security policy for items, such as passwords, account lockouts, and Kerberos settings.

- ◆ You should determine the administrative structure for the domain. This identifies the administrative containers needed to perform network maintenance efficiently.

- ◆ A single domain structure means that the domain name is also the name of the forest root. This name cannot be changed without reinstalling AD.

- ◆ In a single domain structure, users do not have to contact a Global Catalog server to be authenticated nor is there any need for universal groups. This greatly simplifies the security and physical architecture.

- ◆ A very large domain with multiple levels of OUs may need to use security group nesting for efficiency and for easily parsing or reviewing group membership.

- ◆ A single domain structure should still use domain local and global groups in anticipation of future growth.

- ◆ A single domain environment is also used when only part of the organization is prepared to move to the AD domain. In this case, it is important to ensure that the forest root domain name is inclusive of the entire organization to expedite future child domain members.

- ◆ When designing a single domain structure with multiple OUs, try to ensure that the top-level OUs are static. For example, base the top-level OUs on geographic characteristics rather than departmental names that can change in a company reorganization.

OBJECTIVES ON THE JOB

Most organizations should be able to use the single domain structure. Single domain structures are able to have a consistent security policy and a single Windows 2000 and DNS domain name across the entire enterprise. It is also possible for an organization with distinct and independent subsidiaries to create separate forests. Each of these is treated like a single domain.

PRACTICE TEST QUESTIONS

1. **The AD design team for Pharmco is evaluating their network to determine which design structure would best fit their needs. One of the design engineers has suggested that a single domain model would be the best structure. What are some of the reasons why a single domain environment is desirable?**
   a. It is easier to manage than a multiple domain environment.
   b. Delegation of authority only needs to be designed for one domain.
   c. With only one domain, you can have fewer domain administrators and more container or OU administrators. This limits the security privileges that must be assigned to manage the network.
   d. All of the above

2. **Pharmco has developed an implementation plan for AD. Initially, only the forest root domain will be created, and other domains will be added incrementally. What factors need to be considered in this situation? (Choose all that apply.)**
   a. The name of the forest root does not matter because each domain will have its own name.
   b. The name of the forest root domain should be inclusive of the entire organization.
   c. Create an OU administrators group for managing the other domains when they are added.
   d. It is a good idea to create the physical structure once the first domain is created so that additional domain controllers can be added to the appropriate sites.

3. **When developing the group strategy for a design, what goals should be satisfied? (Choose all that apply.)**
   a. Follow the AGLP strategy.
   b. Minimize the number of levels of group nesting to make it easier to track permissions.
   c. Be sure to document the purpose of all the groups so new administrators will be able to understand the group structure.
   d. Create groups wherever users share common characteristics for resource access.

4. **Pharmco has developed an AD domain design that will utilize the single domain model. Each product line will have its own OU so that the application software controlling manufacturer of each drug can be controlled locally. One of the product line managers wants to change the password policy for PCs in his section because he is afraid that the designs for their highly advanced product line will become a target for theft. Can the product line manager implement his own security policy? (Choose all that apply.)**
   a. Yes, an account policy can be assigned to the PCs in the OU, but it will only be in effect when users log on to the PCs using local user accounts.
   b. No, account policy for user accounts on local PCs must be set at the domain.
   c. Yes, account policy for users in the domain can be set at any OU.
   d. No, account policy for users in the domain can only be set at the domain level.

3.7.2 Design an Active Directory implementation plan: Design a multiple domain structure

MULTIPLE DOMAIN STRUCTURE

UNDERSTANDING THE OBJECTIVE

Although many organizations only require a single domain structure, existing security restrictions, size considerations, and other factors may lead a company toward a multi-domain AD structure. Multiple domain structures may be required for technical reasons but are most often created to resolve political concerns.

WHAT YOU REALLY NEED TO KNOW

◆ Additional domains are usually created because the organization cannot agree on a single security policy. For example, some parts of the company may have a need for more frequent password changes or more rigorous account lockout policies. Business units with less stringent security requirements may find frequent password changes and the possibility of account lockouts burdensome.

◆ Group policies that are assigned at the site level inherit down through the entire domain structure of domains within a particular site. Domain administrators, in child domains that are hoping for complete control over computer and user objects, have to limit inheritance from higher-level containers.

◆ Multiple domain structures are used in organizations that have decentralized administration. It allows each business unit to operate as a separate entity while still maintaining transitive trust relationships that enable resource sharing throughout a forest.

◆ In a multi-domain environment, domain administrators in one domain do not have administrative privileges in another domain unless they have administrative privileges in the forest root domain.

◆ Multiple domain structures can also be used when one business unit has dealings with external business partners, and the organization wants to limit their exposure.

◆ Multiple domains are also used to limit replication traffic in organizations that are constantly changing.

OBJECTIVES ON THE JOB

Multiple domain structures require more planning, both for the DNS environment and for the security and administrative environments. Many tasks related to the configuration and schema partitions of AD will be performed by administrators in the forest root domain and will affect the underlying child domains. Therefore, changes in AD logical and physical structures must be coordinated with all the Domain Administrators in the child domains.

PRACTICE TEST QUESTIONS

1. Given the information you have about Pharmco's security requirements, what type of a domain model do they need and why?
   a. Single domain model because it is most efficient
   b. Multi-domain model because of the security requirements
   c. Single domain with multiple OUs because of decentralized administration
   d. Multi-domain and OU model due to security decentralized administration

2. Pharmco has two domain administrators groups: one for the Pharmco.com domain and another for Operations.Pharmco.com. A member of the Domain Administrators group in the Operations domain tries to create a user object in the Pharmco domain and is unable to connect to the other domain. As a domain administrator in his domain, he is able to create user objects. Why is the administrator unable to create the object?
   a. Each domain has its own Domain Administrators group. These groups are identical and have the same permissions.
   b. Each domain has its own Domain Administrators group. These groups are independent and have permissions to objects in their home domain.
   c. Each forest has one Domain Administrators group. This group has rights throughout the entire forest. The administrator must be in a different forest.
   d. Each tree has its own Domain Administrators group. This group has rights throughout the entire tree. The administrator must be in a different tree.

3. Pharmco's Research Division has developed a relationship with Stevenson Institute of Technology that allows students at Stevenson to intern at Pharmco and to assist in the research and development of new drug therapies. This relationship requires the interns and some faculty advisors to access information from the Research Division's file servers. Pharmco's management is concerned that these users may be able to access information on the corporate servers and wants to limit their exposure. What is the best way to accomplish this?
   a. Create a multi-domain AD structure to restrict the Stevenson users from seeing the corporate server objects.
   b. Create a Research OU to restrict users from seeing the corporate server objects.
   c. Create a Stevenson OU to restrict users from seeing the corporate server objects.
   d. Create a Stevenson domain in a second tree in the AD structure to restrict users from seeing the corporate server objects.

4. Pharmco's Operations Division needs at least twelve-character passwords for domain user accounts. The rest of the company can use eight-character passwords. How does this affect the design of AD?
   a. It has no effect on the design of AD.
   b. All users will need to have twelve-character passwords.
   c. Another domain could be created that would allow a separate password policy.
   d. Create another OU for the separate password policy.

3.7.3 Design an Active Directory implementation plan: Design a multiple tree structure

MULTIPLE TREE STRUCTURE

UNDERSTANDING THE OBJECTIVE

A few organizations have the unique situation in which there is more than one distinct company identity. These companies will create a multi-tree structure that derives from unique DNS domain names. These names may originate from existing Internet identities or be based upon product lines that are so distinct as to have completely separate markets, customers, and possibly even unique price structures.

WHAT YOU REALLY NEED TO KNOW

- ◆ A multiple tree structure requires careful configuration of the DNS servers to ensure the proper entries needed to support the unique name. Often, this may mean merging two existing domain name systems into one.

- ◆ The transitive nature of AD translates to the multiple tree structure as well. This means it is equally easy for a user to access a resource in a different tree as it is to access a resource in another domain within the same tree. The first domain controller in the new tree has a direct relationship with the forest root domain.

- ◆ To facilitate the sharing of resources across domain boundaries, Kerberos Key Distribution Centers issue referral tickets to clients that need access to resources in another domain within the same forest.

- ◆ Normally, users follow the path of the trusts as they have been created in the forest to reach a resource in a remote domain. AD allows users to bypass this trust path and establish a much shorter path between domains that share resource information, frequently using a shortcut trust. This can reduce the amount of time it takes to authenticate and access resources in a multiple tree environment in which users would normally have to traverse their home tree up to the forest root domain and then down into the remote tree.

- ◆ Child domains inherit their names from parent domains, leading to contiguous domain names. Domains in different trees have non-contiguous domain names.

OBJECTIVES ON THE JOB

A multiple tree structure should be an unusual event in a Windows 2000 environment. In most instances, it should be possible to create aliases in the DNS servers that service the organization to account for previously used domain name identities. Sometimes, the sheer size and magnitude of an organization drives the reluctance to relinquish a company identity. For example, the Bell Laboratories division of AT&T garnished tremendous respect in the telecommunication community for their engineering successes. Bell Laboratories was almost as well known as the AT&T brand name itself.

PRACTICE TEST QUESTIONS

1. **Pharmco has recently purchased a new subsidiary called Meredith Drugs that has a well-known Internet identity. Pharmco has decided to keep the existing management structure in place at Meredith Drugs and allow them to operate independently. However, Pharmco wants to encourage the Research Divisions at both Pharmco and Meredith Drugs to share basic research and work together on some new shared product lines. How can the AD structure be designed to allow Pharmco and Meredith Drugs to exist as separate Internet identifies while still fostering information sharing?**
   a. Create a multi-domain environment. Change Meredith Drugs' domain name to Meredith.Pharmco.com.
   b. Create a single domain environment. Create a separate OU for Meredith Drugs.
   c. Create a multi-tree environment. The root domain will be Pharmco.com. Meredith Drugs will exist in a separate tree called MeredithDrugs.com.
   d. Create a multi-forest environment. One forest will be called Pharmco.com, and the other forest will be MeredithDrugs.com. Create an external trust relationship between them.

2. **How many DNS servers will be needed to support the domain structure for Question 1?**
   a. Two, with both domains represented on the same DNS server
   b. Two, one for each of two domains
   c. Four, two DNS servers in each domain for fault-tolerance
   d. One, because more than one domain can be created on a server

3. **The Vice Presidents (VPs) in the Research Departments of Meredith Drugs and Pharmco are concerned about being able to share resources if a multi-domain design is implemented. What can you tell the VPs about AD that will alleviate their concerns?**
   a. Shortcut trust relationships could be created between the domains to aid in file access.
   b. AD will automatically create transitive trust relationships between the domains to aid in file access.
   c. External trust relationships could be created between the domains to aid in file access.
   d. AD will automatically create NT-style trust relationships between the domains to aid in file access.

4. **If Pharmco decides to implement a multi-tree structure, what type of DNS names will be used?**
   a. Domain and subdomain names
   b. Parent-child domain names
   c. Contiguous domain names
   d. Non-contiguous domain names

Section 4

Designing Service Locations

System Sciences Corporation

System Sciences Corporation, Inc. (SSC) is a large systems integrator that specializes in helping clients implement new technologies. The company prides itself on offering complete end-to-end solutions, including customized software and appropriately configured hardware. Their latest product has been designed to automate the health club industry, a popular and growing segment of the American business population.

The health club industry is an unusual type of business because most health clubs today combine elements of a membership organization with retail elements. To stay in business in this highly competitive industry, the clubs need to closely manage the needs of the member population. Each club location is run as a separate profit center because the demographics of each location may be different. In one location, the membership may be more interested in exercise classes; in another location, weight-lifting may be the most popular activity; a third location may find high demand for vitamins and supplements.

Active Directory (AD) lends itself well to this type of business because the administrative structure can be delegated to satisfy almost any need. We intend to offer three different tiers of service for the health clubs. The first and second tiers are specialized software for the club locations and the company headquarters. The club software enables each club to monitor all the business activities. Another module allows club members to access their workout information from computer monitors that are positioned adjacent to the various types of equipment, allowing members to look up their records, record their workouts, and track their progress.

The headquarters software connects to the sites and uploads accounting marketing information to enable the corporate headquarters of each health club organization to oversee the clubs in real-time. The analysts at the headquarters can tell the clubs when they need to spend more time with the club participants and which members have been neglecting their workouts. Club counselors can then call the members to determine if there is a problem with club service and resolve any issues that come up. This greatly improves retention.

The third tier of services connects the member system to the Internet. This allows members to access their workout records anywhere in the health club system, regardless of location. Members can access their workout information and update the system with information about their current workout even while away on a business trip or just simply away from home. Club counselors at the remote location can also review the record of the member. If the member tells a counselor at the home club location, a counselor there can send an e-mail message to the remote club to arrange for someone to meet the member and show them around the remote facility.

All these services improve customer satisfaction and dramatically improve the retention rate for health club memberships. In addition, less time needs to be spent courting the members at renewal time. The module that provides the member services is actually part of a network that is run by SSC. The member computers use a different network IP address than the club and club headquarters locations are using. Each health club organization needs to have its own TCP/IP network ID for the computers that comprise the organization's business operations. The network configuration for the member computers will be controlled by SSC. There are several parts of the system that allow the customer, the health club organization, to determine how the system will be configured. For example, DNS services are required for AD to work properly. Client PCs need to have access to DNS services to authenticate to the AD domain controllers. In addition, because health club members can travel to other health club locations and access their personal health club data, Global Catalog servers may be needed to gain access to the AD domain from that location.

Another configuration aspect is whether DHCP will be used and, if so, whether DHCP will be used to populate the DNS servers or whether the DNS servers will be configured for dynamic DNS or secure dynamic DNS. SSC wants to be sure that only health club members and health club staff can access personal information in the member's file. Because health club members, and occasionally staff, are accessing their member information across the Internet, there is a question of privacy. Can the privacy of the information be maintained as it is being sent across the network?

Security is also a concern of the club managers. The information in the member database at their location would be very beneficial to other competing local health clubs. The managers know that competing health clubs send staff to join the club in order to evaluate the level of service that is being provided and to obtain information about service costs. All the competing clubs try to keep their costs and product offerings in the same range to attract new club members. The club managers want to ensure that access to the member services computer system will not compromise the information stored in the business system.

To protect their membership information, the health club organizations do not want member users to be able to display a list of names of all the club members. This means that some of the default security settings for AD may need to be changed so that, although users can authenticate and display information about themselves, the identity of all other members remains anonymous. Members are logged in and out of the club by handing a greeter a membership card when they arrive and retrieving it on the way out. This ensures that only valid members gain access to the club, but it also allows the greeter to pull up the member profile to see when they last purchased supplements or whether they usually purchase an energy drink while they are at the club. If the member does not request these services, the greeter can suggest them. This means that the member's profile is displayed on a computer that could be visible to other club members who come to the desk while the greeter is off creating the energy drink. To avoid displaying this information on the computer screen for long periods of time, this may require the implementation of group policies to the front desk computers that cause a screen saver to cover the monitor after a short period of inactivity.

Each club location needs to be able to create its own users, and each health club organization needs to be able to create its own custom attributes to describe members.

Interviews with Company Employees

CEO - Systems Sciences Corporation seeks to provide the best overall solution for an industry sector. We analyze the business needs of the industry as a whole and create a model that allows enough room for the customization that is inevitable when you are dealing with so many organizations. Our solutions are geared toward maintaining a relationship with the customer and positioning ourselves to continue to offer services after the system installation is complete. Customers can choose to outsource their day-to-day maintenance or establish a support contract for customer assistance or special product modification. These relationships provide additional value to our stockholders because we are able to generate different kinds of revenue. The benefit to the customer is that by the end of the implementation period, we are very familiar with their business operations. This enables us to predict where their environment might be vulnerable and suggest ways to protect against those vulnerabilities.

The goal is to provide value to the customer and assist them in growing their businesses by implementing well-defined system services. The Windows 2000 product line provides a complete solution, and AD allows the product to be customized so that each client's implementation results in the administrative and physical structure necessary to support their organization.

IT Manager - This project is very challenging because as we deploy systems into the field organizations of the customer, the demand on the membership system is steadily increasing. This means we must continually evaluate the membership system to ensure that users always have access to authentication servers, Global Catalog servers, and DNS servers.

The security requirements of the membership system are also peculiar because, although all members need access to the same basic information, we need to protect each organization's private list of members. The AD security requirements are therefore very particular and must be maintained and tested constantly to ensure that users in other organizations cannot see each other's objects. The group policy requirements are relatively stable across each health club organization, so one group policy can be created and linked to other containers.

The system that is deployed to each organization is then customized to meet the needs of the customer. Often the customization includes additional AD attributes or object classes. Although there is an office management system included as part of the package, all member information is contained in AD. This means the other software products are integrated with AD so as to avoid data redundancy. User information is added only once and used by all other system software. Most sites, except for the corporate headquarters of the health clubs, are not large enough to have their own DNS servers. This means the sites must have continuous connections to a remote network segment that contains DNS services.

Health Club Owner - We have 300 locations in large metropolitan areas around the United States. In the past, it has been difficult to gather information about how successful the club counselors, dietary specialists, and personal trainers have been at keeping members satisfied with their workout programs. This new system enables us to gather information from each club location and analyze it to determine which clubs have the most successful programs. Success is measured not by how many members sign up at the health club but by the retention rate. Members who are satisfied with their workout results are much more likely to continue paying dues to the club.

This is also a great marketing opportunity for the organization as a whole. Stress reduction is a great reason for individuals to start a health club membership. However, many people spend a lot of time traveling, and we find that these people tend to drop their club memberships at a higher rate than other types of members. Our IT Department is going to add new attributes to AD so we can track information about members, such as reasons for joining, amount of time spent traveling, and outside interests.

Health Club Office Manager - The network needs to be largely self-administering because we do not have LAN administration staff onsite. The administrators can access the servers remotely across the company WAN and also by dialing in with some specialized software. AD is really just seen as a convenience to our club members so they do not have to carry around their workout cards. Also, we are able to use the software provided by SSC to manage our accounting and office work, like creating brochures for a marketing blitz. The new software helps us track our current members and makes it easier for members to move from one club location to another because their information is available from any location.

The club members can even print out a copy of their workout schedule and track their progress over time. This is a great marketing tool because, if members can see their progress graphically as well as numerically, it gives them the encouragement to stay with their program. In addition, if they are not making as much progress as they would like to, a dietary specialist can assist them in choosing the right products to supplement weight loss or weight gain. Members have very different goals, and having the information available on the computer allows the club to assign each member to a club counselor for monitoring purposes. The only worry I have is that I would not want one of my competitors to gain access to the information in the member database.

4.1.1 Design the placement of operations masters: Considerations include performance and fault tolerance

FSMO • OPERATIONS MASTERS

UNDERSTANDING THE OBJECTIVE

AD has a new domain controller model based upon a system of multiple masters. The multiple master system implies that each domain controller is capable of changing the object database. In a system that permits multiple domain controllers to modify the system simultaneously, certain tasks must be controlled in order to prevent corruption of the AD database. Each domain controller responsible for one of these important tasks is called an operations master.

WHAT YOU REALLY NEED TO KNOW

- ◆ There are five FSMO roles in AD. This does not include the role of Global Catalog server, which is not considered an FSMO role but is almost as important as the FSMO servers themselves.

- ◆ The schema operations master is the single domain controller in the forest with the responsibility for controlling changes to the forest schema. You can improve the performance of schema updates by making changes during times of least system activity.

- ◆ The domain naming master is the single domain controller in the entire forest that has the responsibility for controlling changes to the configuration of AD. This includes adding sites, subnets, site links, or any configuration that changes the physical infrastructure of AD.

- ◆ The infrastructure master also stores information about each new domain controller that is added to AD. When new domains must be created, members of the enterprise administrators group can use NTDSUTIL.exe to add the new domain name before running DCPROMO.exe. DCPROMO.exe can be run by an administrator for the new domain to add the required number of domain controllers.

- ◆ The roles of the operations masters should be distributed so that a failure of one domain controller does not cause a loss of the three domain operations master functions. This is especially important in the forest root domain, in which downtime experienced by the first domain controller created in the domain causes a failure of all five operations master roles.

OBJECTIVES ON THE JOB

The complete name of the special task domain controllers is Flexible Single Master Operation or FSMO. The FSMO function is considered to be flexible because it can be moved from the control of one domain controller to another without compromising system stability. Because these FSMO servers exist, be careful when removing servers from AD. You should always check to see if that particular server holds an FSMO function.

PRACTICE TEST QUESTIONS

1. **SSC has designed an accounting and business management application that integrates with AD. Specifically, the application uses a membership number to track billing and membership status in a health club management package that is accessed by employees at the health clubs and by the Accounting Department at the headquarters of the health club organization. The application causes the schema to be modified. The project designers want to provide guidelines to the technicians that will install the software in the field. Where should the application be installed?**

   a. This is a single forest design, so the application should be installed at the project location at SSC on the AD domain controllers holding the membership information.

   b. This is a multi-forest design, so the application should be installed at the headquarters of each health club organization.

   c. This is a single domain design, so the application should be installed at SSC and pushed to all the domain controllers at each health club over the WAN.

   d. This is a multiple tree design, so the application should be installed on domain controllers in each domain that has a non-contiguous name.

2. **What is an important guideline for the designers to include in their instructions if they want the impact on AD performance to be minimal? (Choose all that apply.)**

   a. Schedule the application installation during the least busy time on the network, so the domain controllers can replicate the AD schema changes quickly.

   b. Schedule the application installation during the least busy time on the network, so the schema operations masters in each domain can replicate the AD schema changes quickly.

   c. Schedule the application installation during the least busy time on the network, so the domain naming masters can replicate the AD schema changes quickly.

   d. Instruct the technicians to run the first part of the application installation, which modifies AD, during a slow time on the network. The second part of the application can be installed any time.

3. **The SSC technicians are scheduled to run the application installation program but have been instructed to ensure that the AD schema operations master is modified to allow changes to be written to the schema. What needs to occur to ensure the schema update can be implemented?**

   a. The Domain Admin must remove R/O permissions from C:\Winnt\System32.

   b. The Creator Owner must remove R/O permissions from C:\NTDS.

   c. The Domain Admins must remove R/O permissions from C:\NTDS.

   d. A member of the schema administrators group needs to change the schema operations to allow the schema to be modified.

4.1.2 Design the placement of operations masters: Considerations include functionality and manageability

OPERATIONS MASTERS

UNDERSTANDING THE OBJECTIVE

Operations master roles exist on only a few domain controllers in each domain because each role can only be represented once in any given domain. Indeed two roles, the schema operations master and the domain naming master, can only exist once in each forest. The other roles, PDC emulator, RID operations master, and the infrastructure master exist once in each domain.

WHAT YOU REALLY NEED TO KNOW

◆ The functionality of the schema operations masters can only be modified by the administrator in the forest root domain or by members of the schema administrators group. By default, the schema operations master is set to read-only, and schema changes are not permitted.

◆ The domain naming master can only be managed by members of the enterprise administrators group, a management group that only exists in the forest root domain.

◆ All the operations master roles are initially contained on the first domain controller created in each domain. The forest root domain contains two roles unique in the forest: the schema operations master and the domain naming master.

◆ The RID master assigns a pool of unique relative identifiers to be used by each domain controller when creating new security principles. Each object must receive a unique security identifier at creation time, and the RID master is responsible for ensuring that domain controllers within a domain have unique RID pools.

◆ The infrastructure master is responsible for maintaining correct references to objects that exist in other domains but are referenced by objects in the domain where the infrastructure master exists. For example, groups can hold references to objects, such as users, that exist in remote domains. If changes occur to this remote object, the infrastructure master is responsible for determining what the changes are and for replicating that information to all the other domain controllers within the domain that hold the membership list of that group.

◆ The PDC emulator receives preferential notification of password changes from each domain controller within a domain and acts as a PDC to domain controllers and downlevel clients not running the AD client.

OBJECTIVES ON THE JOB

It is important to identify which domain controllers in a domain hold the operations masters roles. If these PCs experience downtime, certain domain functions are compromised, and an administrator may need to run special utilities to re-establish one or more of these functions. In addition, it is important to ensure that only members of the domain, enterprise, or schema administrators have the privileges to modify the configuration of these domain controllers.

PRACTICE TEST QUESTIONS

1. **SSC has begun project implementation for a new health club organization called Firm and Tone. Firm and Tone has a headquarters in Dallas, TX, and multiple club locations throughout the southwest. Technicians are ready to install a domain controller for the membership system in the first health club, located in Albuquerque, NM. The technicians are not members of the schema or enterprise administrators groups, and they do not know the password for the administrator account for the root domain. What should be done to allow the technicians to proceed with the installation of the domain controller?**

   a. The domain administrators should perform the installation instead.

   b. The enterprise administrators should perform the installation instead.

   c. A member of the enterprise administrators group should create the domain name in advance, and then the technicians can create a new domain controller.

   d. A member of the schema administrators group should create the domain name in advance, and then the technicians can create a new domain controller.

2. **The technicians implementing the new systems for Firm and Tone are having some problems with the RAID controller on one of the domain controllers. The new controller will not arrive for two days, and the server has failed three times over the past week. The domain controller is holding the RID master role, and the project manager is concerned that the downtime being experienced by the domain controller will cause problems creating new objects in AD. Should the RID master be moved to another domain controller?**

   a. No, the RID master assigns a pool of several hundred RID numbers to each domain controller. Because the RID master is available most of the time, the problem should not affect object creation in AD.

   b. Yes, the technicians should use Active Directory Users and Computers to move the RID Master to a more reliable server.

   c. Yes, the technicians should use NTDSutil.exe to transfer the role to another server.

   d. Yes, the technicians should use NTDSutil.exe to seize the role and specify another server to function as the RID Master.

3. **Firm and Tone has an existing NT 4.0 domain that requires AD to operate in mixed mode for a short time period. SSC technicians have been installing domain controllers and moving the operations master roles to different domain controllers to ensure that the loss of one domain controller will not cause a problem. The project manager is concerned that with so many down level clients, the workload of the PDC emulator will be too strenuous. What could SSC do to reduce PDC emulator tasks?**

   a. Upgrade all downlevel clients to Windows 2000.

   b. Install the AD client on the downlevel workstations.

   c. Upgrade all the downlevel domain controllers to Windows 2000.

   d. All of the above

4.2.1 Design the placement of Global Catalog servers: Considerations include performance and fault tolerance

USERS • APPLICATIONS • UNIVERSAL GROUPS

UNDERSTANDING THE OBJECTIVE

Global Catalog servers are necessary in a multi-domain environment so that users can be authenticated and awarded a security token that contains a complete list of the groups in which they have membership. Global Catalog servers are the only domain controllers in AD that hold the membership list for universal groups and the only domain controllers that have a complete list of all the domain objects in AD.

WHAT YOU REALLY NEED TO KNOW

- ◆ By default, only one Global Catalog server exists in the AD forest. It exists on the first domain controller that is created in AD. To avoid an AD design that contains a single point of failure, configure additional domain controllers to act as Global Catalog servers.

- ◆ Users and applications use Global Catalog servers to find objects that do not exist in their home domains. Global Catalog servers contain only a small subset of attributes for AD objects. This enables the Global Catalog server to quickly fetch the data that satisfies a query.

- ◆ To continue to maintain the speed of query response on a Global Catalog server, keep the list of searchable attributes low. An attribute is replicated to the global catalog if the properties of the attribute have been configured to allow the replication. Most attributes in AD are not replicated to the global catalog.

- ◆ When a user generates a query that uses the Global Catalog server, a response is sent directly to the originator, if the attribute requested is part of the set of information maintained by the global catalog. Each site should have at least one Global Catalog server, so users can satisfy queries in their local site rather than going across a WAN link.

- ◆ The Global Catalog servers hold the membership lists for universal groups. These groups allow users to gain access to resources across the entire forest. If the universal group SIDs is not added to users' access tokens, there will be resources users cannot access and resources to which users can have restricted access.

- ◆ Changes to the membership list of universal groups must be replicated to the Global Catalog servers throughout the forest. You should make changes to the membership list infrequent by adding groups rather than users to universal groups.

OBJECTIVES ON THE JOB

The number of Global Catalog servers available in the AD forest impacts how quickly users can be authenticated. If few Global Catalog servers exist in an environment that is volatile or divided into many WAN segments, users may experience slow authentication times while available global catalog services are identified.

PRACTICE TEST QUESTIONS

1. **SSC has developed an AD design that spans the entire enterprise of Firm and Tone. The design team is analyzing the geographical layout of the physical network and trying to determine how many Global Catalog servers will be required. If Firm and Tone has a multi-site, multi-domain AD logical design, how many Global Catalog servers exist by default?**
   a. One, in the forest root domain
   b. One in each AD domain
   c. One in each site
   d. Not enough information to determine

2. **SSC will be maintaining a membership system for health club members, which allows them to access their health club information from a computer at any health club location that participates in the system. How can SSC reduce traffic across the WAN links that service this application?**
   a. Install a domain controller for each domain at the health club locations.
   b. Install a PDC Emulator at each health club location.
   c. Make sure the domain controllers at the health club locations are also Global Catalog servers.
   d. Make sure there are multiple domain controllers designated as Global Catalog servers.

3. **Health club locations experience a high volume of traffic, much of it from members but also from attendees at exercise classes and prospective members. To prevent access to the application by non-members and to protect the integrity of the data, SSC has implemented NTFS permissions for the application. They want to ensure that all members in the AD enterprise have access to the application, yet they do not want to set permissions for each individual domain. In addition, they do not want a high volume of replication traffic. What is the best way to implement this set of requirements?**
   a. Create a domain local group in each domain, and assign permissions to access the application. Add new members to the domain local groups.
   b. Create a global group in each domain. Use the global group to assign access permissions to the application. Have new members added to the membership list of the global groups.
   c. Create a domain local group in each domain. Create a universal group, and assign permissions to access the application. Add the domain local groups from each domain to the universal group. Have new members added to the membership list of the domain local groups.
   d. Create a global group in each domain. Create a universal group, and assign permissions to access the application. Add the global groups from each domain to the universal group. Have new members added to the membership list of the global groups.

4.2.2 Design the placement of Global Catalog servers: Considerations include functionality and manageability

NTDS.DIT • ACTIVE DIRECTORY SITES AND SERVICES • GLOBAL CATALOG SERVERS

UNDERSTANDING THE OBJECTIVE

Global Catalog servers hold a copy of every object created by an administrator in any AD domain. However, the Global Catalog server does not contain every property of each of these objects. Rather, the Global Catalog server contains a subset of the most frequently accessed attributes that are associated with a particular object.

WHAT YOU REALLY NEED TO KNOW

- ◆ Members of the schema administrators groups determine whether an attribute is contained in the Global Catalog server because only the schema administrators group can authorize changes to the schema. One of the configuration items that can be specified for the AD is the list of attributes that is maintained on the Global Catalog server.

- ◆ The Global Catalog server function should not exist on the same domain controller as the infrastructure master role. This is because the infrastructure master is responsible for determining the changes to objects referenced in other domains. Because the Global Catalog server always contains the most up-to-date information about objects in the entire forest, the infrastructure master never detects any changes and does not maintain referential integrity for the domain as required.

- ◆ The Global Catalog server is a domain controller that contains not only the three full partitions that are normally stored on a domain controller but also another partial, read-only partition containing the domain objects from all domains in the forest. This read-only partition is called the global catalog. All partitions are stored in the NTDS.dit database located in the Systemroot\Ndts directory on domain controllers.

- ◆ A domain controller can be specified to hold the global catalog by modifying the properties of the NTDS Settings object in Active Directory Sites and Services.

- ◆ Domains running in native mode are required to have a Global Catalog server so that users can be properly authenticated in the domain. If there are no Global Catalog servers available, users are able to log on locally. Only the administrator can log on to the network without contacting a Global Catalog server. Users logging from remote domains with user principal names must contact a Global Catalog server.

OBJECTIVES ON THE JOB

The Global Catalog server contains a copy of the primary attributes of every domain object in AD. This differs dramatically from the database contents of all other domain controllers. Because the global catalog knows about all domain objects, it can perform a lookup on certain common attributes and then refer the user to another domain controller in the home domain of the object for more specific information.

PRACTICE TEST QUESTIONS

1. **SSC has developed a specialized application for the health club industry, which includes custom attributes that have been added to AD. The design team at SSC is trying to decide if the custom attributes should be included in the read-only partition of the Global Catalog server. What types of information can help the design team make their decision?**
   a. Determine how frequently users need to search using that attribute.
   b. Determine if the attribute is associated with a large class of objects or a small class of objects. This determines how much additional replication will be caused by changes to this object.
   c. Determine how frequently the values of these attributes change.
   d. All of the above

2. **SSC has begun an implementation project for Firm and Tone, a large health club organization with broad geographical dispersion in the southwestern United States. Due to the physical network infrastructure and some underlying security concerns, Firm and Tone has a multi-domain AD logical structure. Most of the applications are installed and controlled at the organization's headquarters. Recently, there have been several instances in which a user's name has changed, and the change has not been reflected in remote group membership lists. What could be the cause of this problem?**
   a. The infrastructure master is not maintaining referential integrity because it is on the same domain controller as the Global Catalog server.
   b. There are not enough Global Catalog servers defined in the Firm and Tone AD forest.
   c. There are no Global Catalog servers available at the local site where the users authenticate.
   d. There is not enough information to determine the cause.

3. **SSC wants to ensure that global catalog services are available to users at health club locations when they log on to the membership system. Because users frequently log on at remote domains due to travel requirements, all users log on with user principal names. When the user principal name is used in a domain other than the local domain, a Global Catalog server is needed to resolve the name. How can the design team at SSC ensure that global catalog services are available at the local sites?**
   a. Use Active Directory Users and Computers to edit the properties of the domain controller objects in the domain controller's OU.
   b. Use the Active Directory Schema Manager to invoke the check box "Maintain this attribute on the global catalog" for each domain controller at the health club location.
   c. Use Active Directory Sites and Services to edit the properties of the NTDS setting object for all domain controllers at the health club locations.
   d. Use Active Directory Sites and Services to edit the properties of the NTDS setting object for domain controllers in the membership domain at the health clubs.

4.3.1 Design the placement of domain controllers: Considerations include performance and fault tolerance

DOMAIN CONTROLLERS • ACTIVE DIRECTORY SIZER

UNDERSTANDING THE OBJECTIVE

Domain controllers need to be strategically placed in a network environment to ensure that authentication services and AD database access are always available. Authentication services are only part of the logon process. Users also have group policies applied to both the computer and the user objects. The group policy design may have an effect on how many domain controllers are required to provide reasonable performance during the logon process.

WHAT YOU REALLY NEED TO KNOW

◆ When users authenticate to AD, group policies assigned to the user's object are also applied. If a large number of users are authenticating from the same location, additional domain controllers are required to load balance the application of group policies.

◆ Large AD domains, containing thousands of user objects, require additional domain controllers due to the sheer volume of requests. Domain controllers in a large environment may need to be dedicated to just performing domain controller tasks to improve performance when responding to AD requests.

◆ The number of domain controllers in a domain affect the latency associated with replicating changes between domain controllers. The KCC creates a replication topology to replicate information efficiently throughout the entire domain. The greater the number of domain controllers, the greater the latency between the domain controller where the change was made and the farthest domain controller.

◆ Fault tolerance is enhanced by placing at least one domain controller at each site or location that contains users. This way, even if a WAN link fails, the users are still able to log on, receive group policy, and query the AD database.

◆ Use the Active Directory Sizer tool to determine the amount of traffic that will be generated by AD. AD traffic is determined by the number of changes that need to be processed by domain controllers on a regular database. A large database that generates few attribute changes and seldom creates new objects generates less traffic than a smaller database with many changes.

◆ Attribute level replication also improves the performance of AD.

OBJECTIVES ON THE JOB

Domain controller placement can also affect the replication schedule of AD. Domain controllers in the same site replicate approximately every five minutes, whenever a change has been made on a particular domain controller. Domain controllers located in separate sites replicate based upon schedules that are configured by network administrators.

PRACTICE TEST QUESTIONS

1. SSC has implemented an AD domain for the Firm and Tone health club organization and has also installed a member services domain so that health club members can access their workout records from any health club location that is part of the membership network. Many members schedule their workouts after work, and the hours of 4:00 p.m. until 8:00 p.m. are a high volume time at the health club. During this time, the member computers take a long time authenticating users. What is the best way for SSC to improve the performance of the membership system?

   a. Schedule users so that fewer users are authenticating at the same time.
   b. Install additional domain controllers for authentication.
   c. Install additional Windows 2000 servers and start the authentication service.
   d. Install faster member computers.

2. When SSC first installed the membership system, there were only a few health club organizations using the membership system, and authentication services were very fast. Recently, a large and prestigious hotel chain joined the membership service, and the Help Desk is receiving many more calls about how long it takes to be authenticated. What is causing this problem, and what is the best way to correct it?

   a. Users are logging on from more remote sites, and it takes longer to authenticate from these remote locations. Install domain controllers at the remote sites.
   b. The Internet is becoming more congested, and because users are connecting across the Internet, they are experiencing a slow down. Choose an ISP that does not have as many users.
   c. Install a faster network topology at the health club sites.
   d. As more users are authenticating simultaneously, the demand on the domain controllers increases, especially if there are group policies to be applied. Increase the number of domain controllers available to handle authentication services.

3. SSC wants fault tolerance for the membership system in case the link to the Internet goes down. Although it is an unlikely scenario, it is possible for the ISP to suffer occasional downtime. This is especially true when the ISP is switching over to new DNS servers. How could SSC provide fault tolerance for the membership system? (Choose all that apply.)

   a. Install a domain controller from the membership domain at each Firm and Tone location.
   b. Install Windows 2000 servers, and configure them to run the authentication service.
   c. Install Global Catalog servers from the membership domain at each Firm and Tone location.
   d. Install a domain controller from the membership domain at each Firm and Tone location, and configure them to allow logons using cached credentials.

4.3.2 Design the placement of domain controllers: Considerations include functionality and manageability

MULTI-MASTER REPLICATION • DCPROMO.EXE

UNDERSTANDING THE OBJECTIVE

Domain controllers are needed to satisfy a number of requirements in AD. Administrators need domain controllers to manage the objects in the AD database. Users need domain controllers to perform tasks, such as password changes and queries to the AD database.

WHAT YOU REALLY NEED TO KNOW

◆ Domain controllers should be placed close to the administrators who manage them and in the same site as the user community that is serviced.

◆ Domain controller creation differs dramatically from Windows NT. Under Windows NT, the decision to create a domain controller was made at installation time. In Windows 2000, all domain controllers are initially member servers. A domain controller is created when an administrator runs the DCPROMO.exe program that promotes an existing Windows 2000 server to a domain controller.

◆ Domain controllers also participate in a multi-master replication scheme. In Windows 2000, domain controllers are peers, and each contains a copy of the AD database that can be directly modified. When a change occurs on one domain controller, that change is replicated across the AD partition.

◆ Users can have authentication requests processed by any domain controller in the entire forest, even a domain controller in a different domain. This is possible because of the transitive trust relationships that exist between domain controllers in different domains. The domain controller in the remote domain knows how to contact the domain controller in the user's home domain to process the request. The user must either select the appropriate domain from a drop down list in the Winlogon dialog box, or use a user principal name when logging on from a remote domain.

◆ The placement of domain controllers is also determined by the Microsoft services offered in the domain. Exchange 2000 requires a domain controller that is a Global Catalog server to resolve mailbox names. By placing a domain controller holding the global catalog function in each site, the performance of Exchange queries to AD is optimized.

OBJECTIVES ON THE JOB

The number of domain controllers required for authentication services is determined by the number of users that need to log on simultaneously. The network design also affects the placement of domain controllers, if we want to ensure that accessing domain controllers does not dramatically increase WAN traffic.

PRACTICE TEST QUESTIONS

1. **A user from the SystemSciences.com domain wants to log on from a domain called FirmandTone.membership.systemsciences.com. What must the user do to have the authentication request processed? (Choose all that apply.)**
   a. Select the home domain name from the drop down list in the Winlogon dialog box.
   b. Select the local domain name from the drop down list in the Winlogon dialog box.
   c. Use a user principal name to log on.
   d. The user cannot log on from this location.

2. **SSC is setting up an Exchange 2000 e-mail server for Firm and Tone. As the project designers make their final determinations about where to place domain controllers in the Firm and Tone network, one of the project designers brings up the question of Global Catalog servers. How many Global Catalog servers should be suggested to improve performance of the Exchange servers in this network?**
   a. One domain controller that is a Global Catalog server per forest
   b. One domain controller that is a Global Catalog server for each site that has an Exchange server
   c. One domain controller that is a Global Catalog server per domain
   d. One domain controller that is a Global Catalog server per tree

3. **In preparation for supporting the Windows 2000 AD domain being installed by SSC, the network administrators at Firm and Tone Corporation have been engaging in group self-study sessions. No one participating in the groups has been to Windows 2000 training. The network administrators begin to have a discussion about multi-master replication. One of the administrators insists that multi-master replication only occurs after the domain is switched to native mode because, in mixed mode, the job of the PDC Emulator is to replicate to the NT BDCs. Which of the following statements about domain controller replication in Windows 2000 is true?**
   a. In mixed mode, the PDC Emulator performs NTLM replication to the BDCs. Multi-master replication exists simultaneously as the replication method for the Windows 2000 domain controllers.
   b. In mixed mode, the PDC Emulator performs NTLM replication to the BDCs. Multi-master replication does not occur until the domain is switched to native mode.
   c. After AD is installed, only multi-master replication is performed.
   d. None of the above

4. **SSC installed SQL Server 7.0 on a member server and now wants that server to become a domain controller. How can it be converted?**
   a. Reinstall Windows 2000, and select domain controller mode.
   b. Open the properties of the server, and select the button for domain controller.
   c. Move the server from the current OU to the domain controller's OU.
   d. Promote the server to a domain controller by running DCPROMO.EXE.

4.4.1 Design the placement of DNS servers: Considerations include performance and fault tolerance

DATAGRAMS • DNS SERVERS

UNDERSTANDING THE OBJECTIVE

Name resolution services in Windows 2000 are provided by the DNS service. Previous versions of Microsoft network operating systems depended on WINS. This change, from NetBIOS-based name services to TCP/IP-based name resolution services, places a much greater emphasis on a fully functioning DNS implementation.

WHAT YOU REALLY NEED TO KNOW

◆ Users reach DNS servers by sending directed datagrams to a known IP address, so access to DNS services does not rely on special router configuration or broadcasting. This means that users can easily access DNS servers on any subnet in the network, resulting in fewer DNS servers overall.

◆ Because Windows 2000 clients and AD services depend so heavily on DNS for basic network functionality, it is important to have multiple sources of DNS services available in the network at all times.

◆ Users contact DNS servers each time they need access to a TCP/IP resource that is not stored in the local cache on the client PC or in a host file. If resources are widely distributed between many different servers on the network, users need to access DNS servers more frequently. Storing resources on fewer, more powerful servers reduces the number of requests for name resolution and improves the performance of the DNS server by reducing the load.

◆ Users can be assigned multiple DNS server IP addresses. If a primary DNS server does not respond to a DNS request, the next DNS server in the list is contacted.

◆ Using a network of primary and secondary servers, administrators can provide both load balancing and fault tolerance. With just one primary and one secondary server, half the clients in the network can be configured with the primary DNS server as the first server to be contacted, and the other half can be configured with the IP address of the secondary server. This ensures that 50 percent of the DNS requests go to each server.

◆ Converting a DNS zone to an AD Integrated zone also provides both load balancing and fault tolerance because every domain controller with DNS installed has a copy of the DNS zone information.

OBJECTIVES ON THE JOB

The importance of any individual service to a network implementation can be determined by analyzing the result of failures in that service. In the case of DNS, failures can be far-reaching. Users could be unable to locate domain controllers for authentication, administrators could be unable to make changes to the AD database, and services that rely on DNS for passive advertising could be unreachable.

PRACTICE TEST QUESTIONS

1. **Members of the Firm and Tone health club in Houston, TX, log on to an AD domain each time they visit the club for a workout. The domain allows members to access their workout routine and exercise history. The computers the members use are configured to access a DNS server located at an Internet Service Provider (ISP). Because the computers are on a different subnet than the ISP, how can the users' computers access this device?**

   a. Users are not able to access the DNS server because it is on a different subnet than the member computers.

   b. Users are not able to access the DNS server because the member computers need to resolve the name of the DNS server.

   c. The computers can broadcast for the DNS server to contact it.

   d. The computers are configured with the IP address of the DNS server and can send a directed datagram. Name resolution services are not required to contact the DNS server. As long as there is a connection to the Internet, the DNS server can be contacted.

2. **The Help Desk at SSC has started receiving calls from members of the Firm and Tone health club in Houston, TX. The users are not able to log on to the network. A call to the local ISP verifies that one of the DNS servers at the ISP has been crashing all afternoon. What is the best way to change the DNS configuration of the member computers at the health club to correct this problem?**

   a. Install a local DNS server.

   b. Install a local domain controller.

   c. Install a local Global Catalog server.

   d. Change the TCP/IP configuration of the member computers to add the IP address of the secondary DNS server at the ISP.

3. **The ISP that provides Internet connectivity to the Firm and Tone health club has provided the IP address of both a primary and secondary DNS server. If the technicians from SSC are interested in providing both fault tolerance and load balancing for DNS, what is the best way to configure the member PCs?**

   a. Configure the member PCs so the IP address of the primary DNS server is always listed first in the DNS server list of the PCs.

   b. Configure the member PCs so the IP address of the primary DNS server is listed first on 50 percent of the PCs, and the IP address of the secondary DNS server is listed first on the other 50 percent.

   c. The order of the DNS server list does not matter because if one DNS server is busy, the other DNS server is used automatically.

   d. Configure the member PCs so the IP address of the secondary DNS server is always listed first in the DNS server list of the PCs.

4.4.2 Design the placement of DNS servers: Considerations include functionality and manageability

ZONE FILES • SHARED DATABASE • NAMESPACE

UNDERSTANDING THE OBJECTIVE

DNS helps users locate resources in a TCP/IP network. In Windows 2000, DNS becomes a critical service because, without DNS, users cannot perform even the most basic network functions. DNS is an example of a distributed database application because any one DNS server holds only a portion of the DNS hierarchy.

WHAT YOU REALLY NEED TO KNOW

♦ Zone files hold the configuration information about the segment of the DNS hierarchy that a particular server holds. The zone file also specifies whether this is a read-only copy or a copy that can be edited.

♦ Windows 2000 DNS is unique among DNS implementations because zone data can be stored in a shared database rather than in a text file. By configuring a zone to be an AD Integrated zone, information can be changed at more than one location. Each domain controller that has the DNS service installed holds a copy of the DNS zone that can be directly edited.

♦ One of the first decisions your design team must make is whether your network will connect to the Internet. If your organization must connect to the Internet to offer services, you must apply for a registered domain name. That domain name becomes the starting point for your organization's part of the DNS hierarchy.

♦ Organizations that do not offer services on the Internet do not need registered domain names, and the Windows 2000 DNS zone is not advertised on the Internet.

♦ Organizations that do not connect to the Internet at all host a "." domain known as the root domain. The root domain denotes the highest level of the DNS namespace. This is known as a private namespace.

♦ Organizations that must connect to the Internet need DNS servers that can identify Windows 2000 as well as the Internet resources. One way to accomplish this is to use a Windows 2000 DNS server for a private AD namespace and to configure this DNS server for forwarding. There cannot be a "." domain on a DNS server that is forwarding.

OBJECTIVES ON THE JOB

The DNS hierarchy allows the DNS service to operate efficiently. Each server holds a portion of the hierarchy that allows for name resolution of servers in that domain. The top level domains in the DNS hierarchy organize the DNS by business categories. These top level domains divide the DNS database by country, government, military, commercial, educational, private non-profit organization, and Internet service providers using the domain names of US, gov, mil, com, edu, org, and net.

PRACTICE TEST QUESTIONS

1. **SSC is configuring the DNS service to support the corporate AD domain for the Firm and Tone organization. One of the technicians wants to add an MX record for Exchange e-mail services. When he opens the DNS manager on the secondary DNS server, he is unable to add the new record. How can the technician add the MX record from the secondary server?**

   a. The technician cannot add the record from the secondary DNS server because it does not hold a copy of the DNS zone that can be edited.

   b. The technician can change the NTFS properties of the Winnt\System32\Dns\Domain.dns file.

   c. The technician needs to add the name of the primary DNS server to the DNS manager console on the secondary server and change the record on the primary server.

   d. The technician needs to change the security permissions of the DNS server object.

2. **SSC is designing an AD infrastructure for Firm and Tone. Firm and Tone wants to host a Web server to make information about the company available to prospective members via the Internet. However, Firm and Tone does not want to make any of the Windows 2000 resources available on the Internet and wants to protect access to the domain controllers using a firewall. How can the DNS namespace be designed to handle these requirements? (Choose all that apply.)**

   a. Register the domain name firmandtone.com. Have a local ISP handle the DNS services to allow resolution of this domain name and include a host entry for the Web server. Install Windows 2000 DNS, and create a new zone for W2K.firmandtone.com.

   b. Register the domain name w2k.firmandtone.com. Have a local ISP handle the DNS services to allow resolution of this domain name and include a host entry for the Web server. Install Windows 2000 DNS, and create a new zone for firmandtone.com.

   c. Register the domain name firmandtone.com. Have a local ISP handle the DNS services to allow resolution of this domain name and include host entries and all resources including AD resources. Mark the AD resources as hidden DNS records, so they cannot be accessed by anyone on the Internet.

   d. Register the domain name firmandtone.com. Install two Windows 2000 DNS servers for the firmandtone domain, one inside the firewall and one outside the firewall. Add records for all the AD resources to the DNS server inside the firewall. Add a record for the Web server to the DNS server outside the firewall. Forward from the internal DNS server to the external, so internal users can access the Internet.

4.4.3 Design the placement of DNS servers: Plan for interoperability with the existing DNS

DNS IMPLEMENTATION

UNDERSTANDING THE OBJECTIVE

Windows 2000 AD domain services rely on a correctly configured DNS implementation. In many organizations, DNS may already be configured to support an existing TCP/IP implementation. This raises the question of how Windows 2000 fits within the existing namespace and whether to use Windows DNS services or configure the existing DNS servers to support AD.

WHAT YOU REALLY NEED TO KNOW

- ◆ AD requires DNS support for service location records. Service location records are used to register the services being provided by the domain controllers. During the domain controller promotion process, the domain controllers attempt to dynamically register these service location records. Although earlier versions of BIND DNS support service location records, BIND Version 8.2.2 is required to support dynamic registration of the service location records.

- ◆ If a BIND implementation is not Version 8.2.2 or above, the Winnt\System32\Config\Netlogon.dns can be used to create manual service location entries in the zone file that contains the Windows 2000 domain.

- ◆ If the existing DNS implementation does not support the features required by AD, one option is to use Windows 2000 DNS services. Port the existing DNS zone information to the new Windows 2000 DNS server by copying the existing forward and reverse lookup zones to the Windows 2000 server, and placing them in the Winnt\System32\Dns directory.

- ◆ There may be opposition from the existing DNS administrators to hosting the Windows 2000 AD records in the same domain as other DNS records. One option is to have the AD domain hosted in a separate subdomain of the existing DNS implementation.

- ◆ If the existing DNS implementation does not support all the requirements of AD, a subdomain can also be delegated to a Windows 2000 DNS server that can provide all the features that support AD. Once the Windows 2000 DNS server is configured for the AD domain, make one or more of the existing DNS servers secondary for this zone. This can work even if the Windows 2000 DNS server is using an AD Integrated zone.

OBJECTIVES ON THE JOB

If there is an existing DNS implementation, the servers may be administered by UNIX administrators or by the WAN support team. Windows 2000 designers must work closely with the DNS administrators to craft a plan that works for both Windows 2000 and the existing network implementation.

PRACTICE TEST QUESTIONS

1. **SSC is hosting a membership system for the membership of health club organizations throughout the United States. UNIX DNS servers have always provided DNS services for the company's enterprise network. The WAN administrators are reluctant to migrate DNS services to another operating system when the existing system is working so well for all other applications. The current version of the DNS software is BIND 8.2.1; however, the WAN administrators have heard that dynamic registration of service location records does not work with this version. How can the WAN administrators create the service locations records for the BIND DNS servers? (Choose all that apply.)**

    a. The WAN administrators can manually create the records using the information contained in the Winnt\System32\Config\Netlogon.dns file.

    b. The WAN administrators can create the records by cutting and pasting the information contained in the Winnt\System32\Config\Netlogon.dns file.

    c. The WAN administrators can manually create the records using the information contained in the Winnt\Config\Netlogon.dns file.

    d. The WAN administrators can create the records by cutting and pasting the information contained in the Winnt\Config\Netlogon.dns file.

2. **The WAN administrators at SSC have been creating the service location records for the AD domains for six months. This has significantly increased their workload because each time a change is introduced to the Windows 2000 domain, the host and PTR records need to be updated. The WAN administrators do not want to abandon the BIND DNS implementation for the non-Windows applications. What is another way that DNS could be configured that would allow both the UNIX DNS administrators and the Windows 2000 designers to achieve their goals? (Choose all that apply.)**

    a. Make a Windows 2000 server a secondary DNS server for the Windows 2000 zones because Windows 2000 DNS supports dynamic registration of service location records.

    b. Create host files on all the Windows 2000 clients to register the Windows 2000 servers A and PTR records.

    c. Create a delegated zone on the BIND servers, and allow a Windows 2000 DNS server to register the DNS records for the membership domain.

    d. Host the Windows 2000 DNS domains on DNS servers at the ISPs.

3. **Users in the Firm and Tone domain are able to access all the Windows 2000 resources but are unable to access any resources on the Internet. In fact, they cannot reach the Internet at all. What is causing this problem? (Choose all that apply.)**

    a. The users are not configured to use the Internet. They need to go into Internet Explorer and select connect through the LAN.

    b. The Windows 2000 DNS server is configured with a copy of the zone ".".

    c. The Windows DNS server needs to be configured to forward requests it cannot resolve to a DNS server at the ISP.

    d. The users' computers should be configured with two DNS servers, one for the Windows 2000 domain and one for the Internet.

Answer Key

Section 1.0

Objective 1.1

Practice Questions:

1. c
2. a
3. d
4. a, b, c, d
5. a, d, e

Objective 1.2

Practice Questions:

1. a, d
2. b
3. c
4. b

Objective 1.3

Practice Questions:

1. b
2. a
3. d
4. b
5. a

Objective 1.4

Practice Questions:

1. b
2. a, b, c
3. e
4. a, b
5. c, e

Objective 1.5

Practice Questions:

1. a
2. d
3. a, d
4. b
5. c

Section 2.0

Objective 2.1.1

Practice Questions:

1. c
2. b
3. a, c, d
4. a
5. a

Objective 2.1.2

Practice Questions:

1. d
2. a
3. c
4. b
5. c

Objective 2.1.3

Practice Questions:

1. a, b, c, d
2. c (cannot replicate the domain partition using SMTP; default replication interval = 180 minutes)
3. b
4. d
5. c

Objective 2.1.4

Practice Questions:

1. b
2. a, d
3. a, b, c
4. b

Objective 2.1.5

Practice Questions:

1. a
2. c
3. d
4. a

Objective 2.1.6

Practice Questions:

1. d
2. b
3. c
4. b

Objective 2.1.7
Practice Questions:
1. a, c, d
2. c
3. d
4. a

Objective 2.2.1
Practice Questions:
1. d
2. b
3. a

Objective 2.2.2
Practice Questions:
1. b
2. a, b, d
3. d
4. b
5. d

Objective 2.2.3
Practice Questions:
1. LAN Admins - a,d,e OU Admins - b,c,f
2. a
3. c
4. d

Objective 2.2.4
Practice Questions:
1. c
2. a
3. a, b
4. b

Objective 2.3.1
Practice Questions:
1. c
2. a
3. d

Objective 2.3.2
Practice Questions:
1. b
2. d
3. c
4. d

Objective 2.3.3
Practice Questions:
1. d
2. d
3. a
4. c

Section 3.0
Objective 3.1.1
Practice Questions:
1. a, d
2. d
3. c
4. a

Objective 3.1.2
Practice Questions:
1. a, b
2. c
3. d
4. a

Objective 3.1.3
Practice Questions:
1. a
2. b
3. d
4. a

Objective 3.2.1
Practice Questions:
1. a
2. d
3. b
4. c

Objective 3.2.2
Practice Questions:
1. d
2. a
3. c
4. b, d

Objective 3.2.3
Practice Questions:
1. b
2. d
3. c
4. b

Objective 3.3.1
Practice Questions:
1. d
2. c
3. b
4. d

Objective 3.3.2
Practice Questions:
1. a
2. c
3. d

Objective 3.3.3
Practice Questions:
1. b
2. c
3. a
4. d
5. c

Objective 3.3.4
Practice Questions:
1. b
2. c
3. a
4. a

Objective 3.3.5
Practice Questions:
1. c
2. b
3. d
4. a
5. c, d

Objective 3.4.1
Practice Questions:
1. d
2. a
3. b, d

Objective 3.4.2

Practice Questions:
1. c
2. b
3. a
4. d

Objective 3.5.1

Practice Questions:
1. b
2. d
3. a
4. a, d

Objective 3.5.2

Practice Questions:
1. d
2. a
3. b
4. a, c

Objective 3.6

Practice Questions:
1. c
2. b
3. d

Objective 3.7.1

Practice Questions:
1. d
2. b, d
3. a, b, c, d
4. a, d

Objective 3.7.2

Practice Questions:
1. d
2. b
3. a
4. c

Objective 3.7.3

Practice Questions:
1. c
2. a
3. b
4. d

Section 4.0

Objective 4.1.1

Practice Questions:

1. b
2. a, d
3. d

Objective 4.1.2

Practice Questions:

1. c
2. a
3. d

Objective 4.2.1

Practice Questions:

1. a
2. c
3. d

Objective 4.2.2

Practice Questions:

1. d
2. a
3. d

Objective 4.3.1

Practice Questions:

1. b
2. d
3. c, d

Objective 4.3.2

Practice Questions:

1. a, c
2. b
3. a
4. d

Objective 4.4.1
Practice Questions:
1. d
2. d
3. b

Objective 4.4.2
Practice Questions:
1. c
2. a, d

Objective 4.4.3
Practice Questions:
1. a, b
2. c, d
3. a, c

Glossary of Acronyms and Abbreviations

A

ACL – Access Control List
AD – Active Directory
ADSIEdit – Active Directory Service Interface Editor
ARP – Address Resolution Protocol

B

BDC – Backup Domain Controller
BIND – Berkeley Internet Name Daemon

D

DB – Database
DC – Domain Controller
DDNS – Dynamic Domain Name System
DHCP – Dynamic Host Configuration Protocol
DNS – Domain Name System
DSL – Digital Subscriber Line

F

FRS – File Replication Service
FSMO – Flexible Single Master Operation
FTP – File Transfer Protocol

G

GPO – Group Policy Object

I

IP – Internet Protocol
IPSec – IP Security
ISDN – Integrated Services Digital Network
ISP – Internet Service Provider
ISTG – Intersite Topology Generator
IT – Information Technology

K

KCC – Knowledge Consistency Checker
KDC – Key Distribution Center

L

LAN – Local Area Network
LDAP – Lightweight Directory Access Protocol

M

MAC –Media Access Control
MB – Megabyte

N

NetBIOS – Network Basic Input Output System
Netsh – NETSH.exe Network Configuration Tool
NT – New Technology (Microsoft Windows Operating System)
NTDS – NT Directory Service

O

OS – Operating System
OU – Organizational Unit

P

PC – Personal Computer
PDC – Primary Domain Controller

R

RID – Relative ID
RIPrep – Remote Installation Preparation
RIS – Remote Installation Service
RPC – Remote Procedure Call

S

SAM – Security Access Manager
SID – Security Identifiers
SMB – Server Message Block
SMS – Systems Management Server
SMTP – Simple Mail Transport Protocol
SNMP – Simple Network Management Protocol
SQL – Structured Query Language
SRV – Service Records

T

TB – Terabyte
TCO – Total Cost of Ownership
TCP/IP – Transmission Control Protocol/Internet Protocol

V

VPN – Virtual Private Network

W

WAN – Wide-Area Network
WINS – Windows Internet Naming Service